Young Children's Sculpture and Drawing

Young Children's Sculpture and Drawing

A Study in Representational Development

Claire Golomb

Harvard University Press
Cambridge, Massachusetts
1974

To the memory of my mother, Fanny Schimmel Monderer, 1902–1972, and to my enthusiastic daughters, Mayana and Anath, whose early artistic endeavors sparked the curiosity that led to this investigation.

Preface

Children's drawings delight and perplex psychologists, educators, and parents alike. They have been recorded, studied, and used as an indicator of intelligence (Goodenough, 1926). Many a concerned parent or teacher has attempted to correct "faulty" representations, to teach the child the proper placement of parts and the significance of counting the fingers and drawing the right number of limbs.

The persistence of odd configurations such as the "tadpole" drawing has raised intriguing questions. A tadpole drawing consists of a disproportionately large head from which arms and legs sprout. It resembles a caricature of a man. This figure presents a typical example of the peculiar deviancy of children's drawings from adult conventions. Students of children's art have compiled long lists of mistakes in drawings such as omission of parts, faulty placement, lack of perspective, gross disproportion, and disregard for the realistic number of parts and features. In the light of the child's other accomplishments at the age of three to four years— such as the acquisition of language and symbolic play, the solution of formboard puzzles, and the capacity to build with blocks—his drawings are puzzling and seem to reveal a lag in representational development.

The child's first drawings are global configurations which do not resemble the object and lack its most essential attributes. Since, to judge by his behavior, the three-year-old perceives the world veritably, why doesn't he draw what he sees? Since the retinal projection of objects is orderly and accurate, why is his drawing distorted and impoverished? Some early investigators (Sully, 1896) considered drawings mere symbols for reality, while others (Ricci, 1887) adopted a functional approach, interpreting them in

terms of the parts that were important to the child.
Ricci's humorous remark that the child draws all he
needs—head for eating and seeing, legs for walking—
presented a popular point of view and survived for
a long time. Other theorists (Eng, 1931) blamed the
child's mental image, and considered the memory
image which he forms of an object as vague or
confused and somehow responsible for the childish
drawings. The theory eventually adopted and still
invoked most frequently considers the child's drawing
an index of his concept of the object (Goodenough,
1926; Harris, 1963). Reasoning that there must be a
relation between cognition and drawing, a close
correspondence was assumed between drawing,
thought, and language (Eng, 1931; Piaget, 1926,
1956). According to this theory, early drawings
reveal the child's deficient analysis of the object and
his inability to synthesize the individual parts into
a coherent representation. They reflect conceptual
immaturity and are symptomatic of prelogical,
syncretistic reasoning. Thus, in order to account for
the discrepancy between the child's accurate visual
perception and his distorted drawings, the emphasis
was shifted from vision to knowledge. The child
draws what he knows, not what he sees, and he draws
what is most important to him. Once this view was
accepted it was not questioned seriously; data which
did not support it were ignored or screened out.
In the older texts on children's drawings one could
find samples of the child's first attempts to draw a
man consisting of a scribbly representation including
head, body, and legs (Krötzsch, 1917; Burt, 1921; Eng,
1931). This was followed by a "tadpole" drawing,
executed with greater skill although the trunk was
now omitted. Early biographical accounts of children's
drawings provided a wealth of information including
such interesting observations as reported by Lukens
(1896) that young preschool children, hardly past the
scribbling stage, preserved correct spatial localization;

Young Children's Sculpture and Drawing

he defined this period as "the period of local arrangements." Other reports stressed the child's critical attitude toward his finished work and his exploratory orientation toward the medium.

Recently the now classical theory which considers children's drawings as an index of their conceptual immaturity has been reevaluated from the perspective of a psychological theory of representation. In *Art and Visual Perception* (1954) Arnheim analyzed the relation between perception and representation and distinguished between concepts of representation and of imitation. He rejected the notion that reality can be copied and defined the process of artistic representation as a search for structural equivalences of form in a given medium. The child, as well as the adult artist, does not attempt to copy reality; his task is to invent structurally adequate forms which can stand for the complex object. Arnheim pointed out that the shapes the child uses in drawing, the first circles and lines he produces, are not provided by the object; they are created by the child and thus are his genuine inventions.

When the drawings are considered from the vantage point of this theory of representation, the developmental sequence becomes comprehensible and the apparent contradictions which perplexed earlier students of children's art can be resolved. So long as psychologists held the naive view that reality could and should be copied, they were merely concerned with replication and its deficiencies. The absence of realism or naturalism in early drawings of children required an explanation; it was considered an imperfection to be corrected in due time by progress in conceptual development. Thus, children's drawings were evaluated in the light of historically and developmentally late accomplishments such as realism in art. From this perspective they appeared to be faulty imitations, lacking the most essential attributes of the object. The belief that a drawing consists of elements "copied from reality" and that conceptual development can be measured by adding the separate elements and counting the number of represented parts was directly derived from psychology's empiricistic heritage.

In 1969, in an extensive doctoral dissertation, I addressed myself to the issues raised by the two opposing theories of graphic representation. The overall results supported Arnheim's theory and provided experimental evidence for the existence of multiple determinants rather than point-for-point correspondence between the child's drawing and his concept of a man. I rejected the hypothesis which assumes a simple form of parallelism between knowledge of the object and its representation. This investigation was subsequently expanded to include modeling of the human figure (Golomb, 1972), to study the origins of representation, and to follow the transition from prerepresentational activity to the invention of universally meaningful forms.

This book attempts to trace the development of the human figure in two different media, drawing and modeling. Emphasis is placed on the evolution of the sculpted man, which has never been adequately documented. The study of the birth and growth of the human form is presented from a developmental point of view and bears both on child psychology and on the early history of art. Its specific aim is to chronicle the representational sequence and to compare the evolution of the human figure in the two- and three-dimensional media. While this book offers a general outline of progress in representation and within very broad limits provides norms, it also attempts to show how varied and inventive the young child's productions are at each stage of development.

The sculptures and drawings were solicited by an adult. This was done in order to record the *process* of

Young Children's Sculpture and Drawing

creation and to take account of the verbal remarks which freely accompany the child's work. Had I restricted myself to purely "spontaneous" creations, my information would have been limited to the end result and the records of observation would have been incomplete. Since the final product is often quite ambiguous in structure and content, the value of such work would have been questionable. Moreover, the existence of truly spontaneous representations in nursery schools is debatable, since the very provision of materials such as paper, crayon, playdough, or plasticene implies an invitation to use them, and thus a task is set. Furthermore, children learn from each other in the nursery school or at home as they play with the materials and discover what can be done with them. From a comparison of children's representations, created on their own initiative or on request, it appears that children's spontaneous exploration of the two- and three-dimensional media follows a course similar to that induced by the invitation "to make" something. Though requesting can be construed as an intervention, a prodding, evidence does not point to any significant formal differences in the results. Work-on-request may represent the child's optimal performance. The advantage of the controlled situation is considerable since it enables us to record the child's efforts, to observe the process of creation, and to better understand the outcome. The data obtained in the standardized experimental situation may be considered as a fairly representative sample of the developmental sequence in modeling and drawing.

Throughout my contacts with the children I attempted to establish friendly relations with them, to encourage, show approval, and praise their work. As part of the standardized instructions each youngster was promised a present of playdough upon completion of the task. The children were enthusiastic participants and spontaneously lined up outside my office to get their turn at "playing." The very youngest, aged two years and four months to two years and eight months, were an exception. They did not quite comprehend the request "to make something" and some may have felt uneasy about the situation. A few of these youngsters wanted to leave as soon as possible and return to their nurse and playmates. Others played with the dough, smiled at the experimenter and were quite happy with their little present of playdough.

The study was conducted in the United States and Israel; subjects ranged from two to seven years and were drawn from prenursery, nursery, kindergarten, and first-grade classes. Each child was presented with a portion of playdough and asked to make the following objects: a doll, a mummy, and a daddy. Subsequent to modeling, the youngster was offered paper and crayons and asked to draw a child, a mummy, and a daddy. This task was followed by the instruction to draw a man on dictation. Altogether, three hundred children were tested in individual sessions and extensive protocols recorded. Several additional representational tasks were given to approximately half of the subjects; these included the graphic completion of an incomplete figure, the construction of a puzzle man, and the modeling of a snowman.

This book concerns itself with the evolution of the structural characteristics of the human figure; no attempt has been made to assess potential psychodynamic aspects of the representation.

The discovery that representational forms evolve in a universal pattern, intimately related to the child's cognitive development, has tempted psychologists to search for analogous principles relating the child's drawing to unconscious personality dynamics, in particular his self-image (Buck, 1948; Machover, 1949; Bender, 1952; Hammer, 1968; Koppitz, 1968). Machover was one of the first psychologists to propose a set of systematic relationships between a person's drawing of the human figure and the image he has of himself. Such characteristics as the size and placement of the figure, completion or omission of features, pressure of line, shading of body and limbs, and erasures were said to be signs of unconscious personality characteristics, of needs, affects, and motives closely related to the person's self-image.

The search for an interpretive key to the child's self-portrait has led to a great deal of research. Swensen (1968), in a thoughtful review of the literature on this subject, concluded that as far as children were concerned the evidence of body image projection in their drawings of the human figure was negative. He suggested that the drawing of a person may reflect different processes for children than for adults. Thus, while the child's individuality and originality clearly come to the fore in his drawings and sculptures, generalizations concerning personality characteristics are tenuous at best: for this reason I have avoided them in this book.

It is with a deep feeling of gratitude that I want to thank my friends and teachers Professors Marianne L. Simmel, Rudolf Arnheim, and Ina Samuels, who generously gave of their time reading the manuscript. Their valuable editorial suggestions and critical comments helped improve the final version of this book. Special acknowledgement goes to my husband Dan, who photographed the fragile sculptures and thus preserved them. He actively encouraged this work from its inception, and without his interest and support this book would never have been written. I wish to express my sincere appreciation to our secretary of the Psychology Department, Mrs. Katharine Chernosky, for typing this manuscript.

C.G.

Fall 1973
Brandeis University
Waltham, Massachusetts

Preface

Contents

PEOPLE

Foreword by Rudolf Arnheim

Modern art has opened our eyes to a better understanding of the work of children. In the presence of painting and sculpture such as that of the cubists it was no longer possible to conceive of man-made images as being derived from their models by a kind of glorified duplication. Idealization, abbreviation, exaggeration were no longer sufficient to account for the startling differences between the signifier and the signified. There was need for a radical turnabout which made us realize that art is not the result of nature transforming itself into images with the help of man, but that images are indigenous responses of the human mind to what it observes in the world of visual experience. The base of departure for image-making was the mind and the body of man with their particular resources, idiosyncrasies, and skills. If one wanted to understand where images came from, one had to look at the makings of the human mind.

Soon it became evident that man-made pictures display their distinctive character best not when they closely resemble the objects they represent but when they keep far away from them. This drew attention to the sources of art in primitive man and in the work of children. The carvings and decorations of the savages, tucked away in the dusty showcases of ethnological museums, and the scribbles of children on walls and pavement and on scraps of paper were examined with new respect. And while artists like Paul Klee and Jean Dubuffet in their works paid homage to the striking directness of expression in these products of the young mind, the literature on child art multiplied and matured.

Claire Golomb's investigation distinguishes itself not only by the new techniques she employs systematically—such as the comparison of pictorial and sculptural work or the dictation method—but by her adherence to the new psychological approach of which I spoke. Enchanted with the rich imagination of the child, she analyzes those simple but infinitely varied figures not by what they lack but by what they offer. And instead of extracting a few rules from highly digested material she presents the reader with the much fuller experience of art work as an exuberant, noisy activity of body and mind, in which producer and product are still inseparable. The vexing problem of what the child actually sees in, and intends by, the spare shapes he draws and models is greatly clarified by what we learn about the child's own spontaneous comments. If we realize that the incompleteness of these representations does not derive simply from inability and ignorance but from the child's awareness that a picture can be valid even though it is not mechanically faithful, our respect for the child's intelligence is newly increased. The announcement: "I don't have to make the nose!" proclaims the independence of a mind not limited to imitation, a mind that observes, judges, selects, and interprets.

The procedure of dictating to the child the parts of the body he or she is asked to represent on paper or in clay may be met with some hesitation by art educators who frown upon any interference with the spontaneity of the child. Such hesitation, amply justified by the harmful effects of overly directive teaching methods, would seem to be unwarranted in the present case. The experimenter prescribes what the child shall do, not how he shall do it, and the results are enlightening not only because of what they tell us about the potential range of the children's ability but also by what they refuse to do and cannot do. Their integrity proves to be quite robust.

Golomb's approach is in line with the renewed interest of psychologists in cognitive processes. She views art work as a valuable means by which the child orients himself in a complex environment. To draw or to model a human figure helps to understand man, at however simple a level. She is concerned with the stages of cognitive development in the visual sector of the mind and with the influence of the two-dimensional and three-dimensional media on the form that cognition takes.

Such studies are badly needed to complement the "projective" approach, that is, the analysis of art work as an expression of motivational forces and emotional attitudes. Too often, clinical psychologists and educators risk misinterpreting features of formal development as personality indicators. Needless to say, one cannot do justice to an individual child's work or indeed to children's art in general without considering the interplay between the motivational and the cognitive forces of the mind. But in order to master the complexity of this task, we need to clarify the workings of the particular components by the kind of solid exploration of which the present book is a welcome example.

Young Children's Sculpture and Drawing

Beginnings

Scribble pictures have customarily been considered forerunners of children's interest in drawing and painting. Tracing representational development back to its modest beginnings, we gain the necessary perspective to follow the evolution of forms, the difficulties of creation, and the joys of accomplishment.

The motor activity in which the scribbling child engages differs from his fascination with "making pictures," which comes later. In the pure scribble stage motor joy rules supreme and the child is unconcerned with the "looks" of the final product, though he is generally pleased that his vigorous motions leave visible marks on the paper. At this stage he is primarily engaged in an action, and representational intention or pictorial possibilities simply do not exist. The scribbles of the two-year-old are clumsy, uncertain marks; the youngster holds the crayon in his fist and frequently pokes it through the paper. In modeling playdough or plasticene he holds the material passively, turns it aimlessly, or hits the table with it. At times he uses playdough in conjunction with other toys, sticking it on blocks, cars, and the like. At this point he does not make any attempt to manipulate the material deliberately.

A few months later, however, between the age of 2-8 to 3-2* the child who continues to play with paper and crayon will produce his scribbles more energetically and more skillfully. He begins to create more articulate forms and to produce an assortment of whirls, lines, and zigzags. He seems increasingly delighted with the motor activity and displays pride in the visible results. In modeling the child now handles the material more actively; the dough is fingered, pounded, stretched, pulled apart and joined together, hammered on the table or on a board. Other actions include patting, stretching, folding,

* In this text the convention of representing years by the first and months by the second numeral has been adopted.

squeezing, lengthening, poking, pinching, and flattening the dough with the palm of the hand. Finally, the child discovers the rolling motion, rolling the dough back and forth on the tabletop, which yields the first visually coherent and pleasing unit in playdough—a truly significant achievement. Altogether his repertoire of actions performed on the playdough has expanded considerably, and without planning he has modeled his first articulate shape in this medium, that is, the rolled dough-snake. The material, however, continues to be handled mainly for its own sake, for the pleasure the child derives from playing with this pliable medium. Though playdough does not lend itself to the creation of such exciting visual forms as scribble motions produced on paper, it boasts of other advantages; it feels mushy-soft and can be thrown about, bounced, rolled on the floor, and pounded energetically.

The scribble and playdough formations described so far are the result of prerepresentational actions devoid of any representational intention. Further practice with crayon, paper, and playdough leads to better and more expressive forms in the two media. These interesting forms capture the child's attention, and he begins to take a closer look at his creations, examining them with curiosity, attempting to discover some likeness in the scribble-picture or playdough-blob. One now observes that the child displays a new attitude toward his work and, for the first time, seems to experience a dawning awareness of forms and of the possibility to make things. This sets the stage for "romancing," which consists of telling stories when pressed by an adult to account for the scribbles. Children "make up" stories to "make" something of the scribbles. For the young three-year-old it can be an upsetting experience to be faced with a task of drawing a man not knowing what the crayon will produce. Romancing, which is a kind

Young Children's Sculpture and Drawing

of forced interpretation of the scribble-picture, presents a way out of the dilemma. This is usually done on the basis of an accidental formation. Romancing takes off from a scribble or playdough-blob, but the narrative develops quite independent of form quality. The mark on the paper or the arbitrarily shaped lump of dough only provides a starting point for the narrative which creates the object or imaginary event. The interpretation is not yet tied to a perceptual likeness. Adopting Piaget's conceptual framework, romancing might be considered an instance of pure play, with little accommodation to reality.

Hilary (3-6), for example, responded to the request to draw a person with a scribble-picture extending over the whole sheet of paper. She explained her drawing in the following manner: "It's a person with a lot of hair—he is having a shampoo." As she talked about the picture she pointed toward rather indistinguishable scribbles and enumerated a list of several body parts including eyes, nose, mouth, body, and legs. She carefully preserved the correct relationships between the "parts" and their approximate location. When asked to make a man of playdough she replied: "I can't make it, but I can make a real big walrus; I know what that looks like . . . [all the while pushing and pulling the playdough into an amorphous lump] . . . I can make a bird [three pieces of dough were flattened on the table] . . . a head, a mouth, forehead, eyes." The examiner questioned "Is that a man?" Hilary replied: "Yes, it is a bird; here are wings, the mouth, eyes, eyebrows, . . . I can make a pig." Following these verbal flights of fancy she rolled the playdough for the first time with the palm of her hand in a back and forth motion and exclaimed: "I made a carrot! I'll make a big ball of all the playdough . . . I made a big fat pancake."

Gina's (4-0) response to the request to make a man was negative: "I can't, too difficult." Meanwhile she handled the dough, rolled it into a ball, talked about her doll, about a television character, and finally about the task itself. "I'm gonna make a baby, a very small one, one year old, then it grows to be two," adding some more playdough to the lump in her hand to indicate the growing baby.

Bobby (3-11) drew zigzag and curved scribbles over his paper, completing his drawing with large swirling forms. He interpreted his picture as follows: "It's a big doll sitting there; I'll make a daddy-animal too."

Abe (4-4), given a portion of playdough, was asked to make a man. He held the blob up in the air and designated the top part as head and the lower part as the legs. However, in the face of the shapeless lump of dough he could not sustain this interpretation for long, and regressed to a romancing attitude: "He takes a bag of stones, maybe I can pat it down to make it smoother . . . Here is a boy riding a horse."

The child does not always give in to the pressure of the task and of the experimenter. Some children hold out, either by plain refusal, by acknowledging that it does not look like anything, or by such tactics as "it's gone," "I made it already," "it's hidden." They refuse to be drawn into an assignment which is beyond their capacity and which does not lend itself to a reasonable solution; they refuse to pretend cooperation. A four-year-old boy was offered some playdough and asked to make a doll. He picked the lump up, turned it in his hand, and inquired: "How do you make a doll?" He continued to turn the dough, pulled a piece off, shaped it lightly between thumb and index finger, rolled it in the palm of his hand, rolled it on the tabletop, pounded the dough, flattened it, pulled some more pieces off the bulk, hammered it with his fist, removed it from the table to his hand, added some more dough, pounded it again, pressed his fingers around it, and finally rolled a snakelike

Young Children's Sculpture and Drawing

shape. The examiner was delighted and asked what he had made. Resisting the temptation to call it a "doll" and be finished with the assignment, or to romance his way out of the dilemma, the boy answered cryptically "something." He was not going to give an arbitrary response in order to gain approval or to pretend that he had solved the problem.

Another four-year-old took the dough, pressed it a bit, and, when questioned about his work, stated without great conviction: "It's a bed for a dolly, the doll is inside." The examiner was not ready to give up and offered the child a new portion of dough with the request that he make a doll. The boy pressed it lightly, pulled the sides up, and pointed to a tiny crack in the dough form: "See—here is the dolly." Then, evidently unwilling to sustain this pretense, he gave up. The game was finished and he acknowledged: "I can't do it, it doesn't work."

The three-dimensional medium fosters a form of interpretation specifically related to actions performed on it. Thus, children bounce a piece of rounded dough in imitation of a ball, move a blob of dough across the table like a train or car, walk a man over the table, and flatten lumps of dough in imitation of meatpatties or pancakes. These are actions in lieu of representation or as an aid to it. They are not performed in order to create a perceptual likeness to the object; rather they imply the object by imitating one of its functions. Ziv (3-2) moved the dough from hand to hand. He squeezed, pulled, turned, and finally flattened it on the table with a pounding motion. Pounding the dough was a newly discovered action, and with great excitement he exclaimed: "a hamburger." Other children may go through similar actions and name the flattened dough-piece a "pancake." The specific action on the dough as well as the suggestion of the shape contributed to the creation of the object. A similar case can be observed

in the modeling of "balls." Abner (4-3) was offered
some dough with the instruction to make a man.
He rounded the dough into a sphere, bounced it on
the floor declaring "a ball, I think it would bounce."

Romancing and imitative actions serve as
substitutes for representation proper and are
pseudo-representational devices to meet the demands
of the task. They mark a transitional stage of
development, when the request to make something is
vaguely understood, even though the child does not
have the faintest idea how to go about it. He knows
only that the adult and the older sibling can "make"
things, and he has an inkling of representational
possibilities, though he lacks functional
representational concepts and models. Thus, if the
child agrees to make a picture for the adult he cannot
do much more than produce a scribble picture. Left to
his own devices—free to scribble as he desires—he
will not spontaneously *name* his scribbles or call
them people. When pressed to interpret his
scribble-picture to the inquisitive adult, the child may
resort to romancing while attempting to maintain
some order in the spatial identification of the parts.
This usually takes the form of locating the head in
the top section, the body in the center of the scribble,
and the legs somewhere at the bottom. At times,
while romancing about the scribble-picture, the child
may forget the beginning of the story and produce
wild confabulations. This, however, occurs rarely and
usually results from undue pressure exerted by an
adult which forces the child to escape from the
situation by resorting to fantasy and ridicule. On the
whole, romancing as an interpretive act seems typical
of a brief transitional phase only, between
matter-of-fact scribbling, refusal to comply with
something the child knows he can't do, and the sober
assessment that it "doesn't look like anything."
Romancing is a fleeting moment in the developmental
sequence and, like action-imitation, is discarded

Young Children's Sculpture and Drawing

fairly soon and replaced by more adequate representational means.

Further along in development from prerepresentation to representation proper we find the somewhat more advanced interpretation of "reading-off" and "verbal designation." Reading-off can best be described as an effort to read the hidden meaning off the scribble-picture or the playdough-blob. It is an interpretation offered *after* the fact of scribbling or working on the dough. It is an incidental discovery of perceptual similarity. The specific assignment is ignored and the accidental product determines its meaning. When the child feels obliged to account for his work, reading-off what the scribble stands for is a sensible approach and reveals a new interest in forms and their recognition. The cumulative benefits of practice with scribble- and dough-forms has led to the recognition of forms, which in turn fosters representational interest. Indeed, the prerepresentational stage ends with the discovery of forms and their creation by the child. Reading-off is a somewhat more advanced invention than either romancing or action-imitation, since it is tied to the "looks" of the product and is not quite as arbitrary and fanciful as romancing. Thus, the three-year-olds who produce overlapping and intersecting circular and squarish forms, which are far more articulate than the earlier scribbles, tend to search these configurations for meaning and may call them "butterfly," "kite," or "ribbon."

Ohad (3-6) drew a pear-shaped form with a small head on top. Upon inspection of the figure he declared that it looked like a "fish," and promptly drew the "sea" in the form of scribble-lines around his fish. Another boy (3-8) questioned the examiner: "How do *you* do it?" After a few encouraging remarks he drew a rectangular form, added two verticals inside it, and remarked, "came out a closet." His next attempt ended in a similar configuration:

"another closet." The third trial resulted in an open rectangle which he filled with two eyes, a nose, and a mouth. He looked at it attentively and noted: "came out a cowboy; no—it is a mask."

Thus, the novel activity of reading-off makes the outcome of scribble-drawing meaningful to the child. In this sense it is an intelligent interpretation of the scribble-picture, and can be considered an accommodation to reality.

"Verbal designation," the most advanced of the pseudo-representational devices invented by the child, is a useful aid to representation since it substitutes verbal parts for modeling or drawing, thus providing the necessary details of the figure. The intention is sustained throughout the process of modeling or drawing, and the designation follows the predetermined goal. The interpretation no longer depends on the dough-form's chance appearance; rather the figure is made to conform to the original intention. Sammy (4-0) was given a portion of playdough and asked to make a man. In turn he fingered, pulled, pressed, pinched, and finally indented it. All these manipulations left the dough rather shapeless, but Sammy maintained that he had made a man and proceeded to "name" the parts while pointing at the figure: "This is the head, this is the nose, this is the hair." Jay (3-9) lengthened her dough portion by pulling and stretching. Next she stood the column-figure up: "It's a mother; she has a breast and a belly." She seemed to study her figure and discovered some ready-made marks in the dough which she called eyes, nose, and mouth. Ramy (4-7) squeezed and pulled his dough-portion into the shape of a column. He stood it up on the table and explained spontaneously: "his head, tummy, legs."

These very crude, elongated and upright standing figures seem to require further definition and to provoke verbal designation of the parts. This solution, however, is not uniformly applied to the column-figure. Some children seem to emphasize the parts which the figure lacks. Eyal (3-10) took the blob of dough, pulled and stretched it a bit, and remarked: "Could be like this here, he has no eyes, and no mouth. You have to pull them [legs] out." His friend (3-9) drew an outline figure resembling a mountain: "I made a big boy but without the head. I don't know how to make one with a head." Benny (3-10) modeled his dough by pressing, pulling, and stretching. "He is big and strong, here is a man, here is his hat [pointed to the upper part], here is his mouth [made a mark] . . . you can close his mouth, his feet I'll pull out, has no arms."

In drawing we find fewer instances of spontaneous verbal designation than in modeling. This may reflect the relative ease or difficulty of representing in the two- or three-dimensional medium. The drawing medium seems to facilitate articulation of expressive qualities, and the first humans, though consisting only of a large circle with facial features, are self-evident configurations. Thus, the drawn figure has a sufficient number of defining characteristics such as the facial features; unlike the modeled man it requires fewer verbal aids. However, the trunk is not yet graphically depicted but merely implied in either head- or leg-space. This type of implication is akin to the verbal designation of parts in modeling.

In the process of exploring his scribble- and playdough-shapes the prerepresentational child develops a growing awareness that lines can "look" like something, in fact contain forms and meaning. Since he lacks representational tools, the child avails himself of pseudo-representational tactics. Accordingly, he relies mainly on verbal aids to interpret the scribble or playdough creation. Verbal means, however, will not satisfy his representational urge for long, and he will search for better means and invent suitable representational forms.

Beginnings

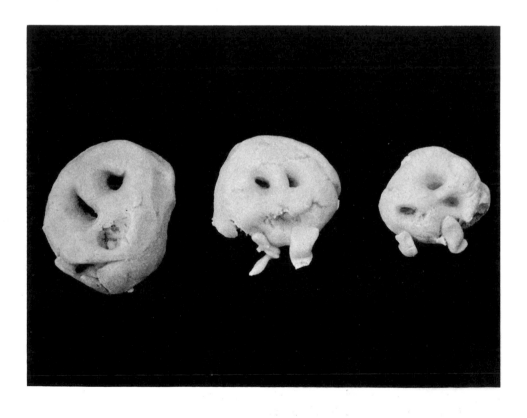

The age of three marks a turning point in the development of representation. Youngsters show an eagerness to explore the media and a capacity for fast learning. The child moves from unruly scribbles to a simple but articulate representation of forms. Once he discovers forms in his scribbles, he is ready to recognize the representational function of lines. In drawing, this stage coincides with the evolution of a circle or ellipse, cleared of the whirls that used to fill the scribble pictures. The circle is a bounded form of "thing" like or "object" quality. The circular contour is not perceived as a line belonging impartially to the inside as well as the outside area; it bounds the *inside* area, which acquires a figural quality and looks more solid than the surrounding field. A selective principle is at work: the line belongs to the enclosed figure and segregates it from the surrounding field (Rubin, 1931; Koffka, 1935). In the circle the child discovers an effective tool to create figures and objects. The use of the clear and single line is also a significant achievement, and some children tend to use it instead of the circle. For representational purposes, however, the line is an ambiguous form, both one- and two-dimensional in character (Arnheim, 1954).

From prerepresentational interpretations and the creation of shapes the child has moved to the discovery of similarities and the invention of simple forms of equivalence. He has acquired skills and evolved his first representational concepts. Even then, minimal forms suffice for many objects. A big circle, oval, or irregularly shaped outline can stand for the person, including head and body in a sweeping enclosure. A smaller circle serves for eyes, nose, mouth, and bellybutton. Other objects such as flowers and animals are also conveniently represented by the circle. The circular shape seems to be favored

Exploration of Forms

by eye and hand and provides a satisfactory solution to initial representational ventures.

Now when the child sets out to make a picture of an object, he has representational means at his disposal, and the simple circle and lines serve him well. The complex coordination of intention, action on the medium, and the looks of the final product is a difficult task. The young artist must sustain his intention throughout the intricate process of creating forms and recognizing the outcome of his efforts as the figure he set out to make. He is engaged in his first attempts to invent suitable representational models. Three early graphic models can be distinguished: the circle-oblong with facial features; the linear configuration; and the depiction of single features.

The child's first and most frequently used representations of people are huge circles covering a large part of the paper and leaving little space for additions. These circular forms, which enclose the inside area, invite further experimentation. The child fills the circle with facial features, bellybuttons, and other embellishments. The outline stands for the *whole* person, though usually only the facial features are graphically differentiated (see Figure 1). The "bounding" characteristic of the circle is a genuine invention as can be seen in those cases where the contour is only partially complete or has been omitted altogether. Some children use the edges of the paper as outline, filling the sheet with such facial characteristics as eyes, nose, mouth, eyebrows, and even arms. The paper serves as background for the graphically differentiated parts and is included in the figural representation. Paper-as-medium provides continuity between parts. Figure 2 illustrates these first representations of a man.

A few examples will help clarify the child's representational conception. Anath (3-8) drew an

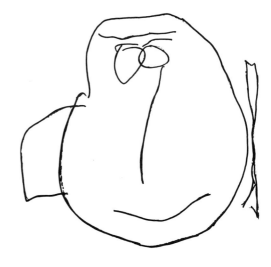

incomplete or "open" circle. Inside she added three smaller circles and two lines, representing eyes, nose, and mouth. She was asked for a second drawing and explicitly instructed to draw the whole person: "This time make a mummy, all of her." Anath used the same graphic model and procedure as before, but the figure became twice as large. When asked if the drawing had a body, she pointed toward the circular outline and stated that this *was* the body (Figure 2a). Jay (3-11) agreed to draw a man. He drew a large circle and added facial features, hair, and ears. He then was given another sheet of paper and instructed to "draw the *whole* person, not just the head." Jay drew a larger circle, this time extending the outline over the whole paper. Again he filled in the facial features, hair, and ears (Figure 2b). Sara (3-9) drew a circle with many folds and stated: "This is his whole big body; I'll draw the eyes too" (Figure 2c).

David (4-6) drew his person in the following manner. He started with a huge outline, closely following the edges of the sheet of paper. In the upper

1. Global human figures. The circle with facial features represents one of the earliest graphic models of the human figure (girl 3-3, boy 3-8).

Exploration of Forms

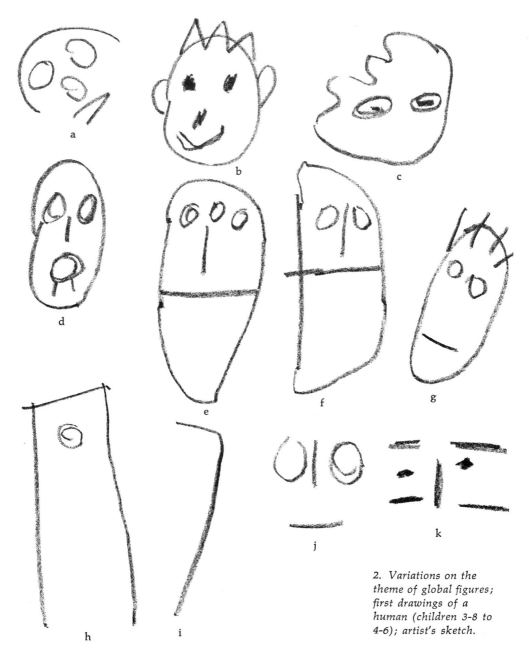

2. Variations on the
theme of global figures;
first drawings of a
human (children 3-8 to
4-6); artist's sketch.

Young Children's Sculpture and Drawing

part he drew two eyes, a nose, and a mouth; in the
center he added a small body with arms and legs
(Figure 3).

The linear model, less frequently employed,
consists of a vertical line drawn across the sheet of
paper, at times extending from the top of the page to
its bottom (Figure 2i). A modified version is the
wavy line with a small circle-head at its end. Another
variation of the linear model is the "open rectangle"
with the eyes drawn in the top section. Eyal (3-10)
provided an example of the rectangular model. He
made three attempts to draw a man. The first time he
said: "you make a line, two lines. But I don't know
how to make a man. You need a long and big line—

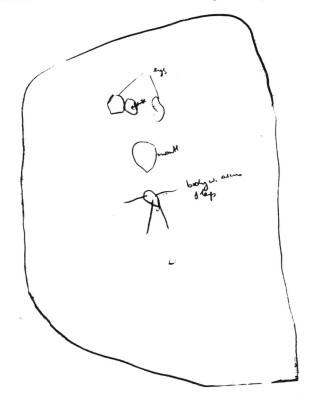

3. *Global figure. Graphic
differentiation of parts
is limited to the inside
area of the contour
(boy 4-6).*

Exploration of Forms

is that how you make a mouth?" (He drew a circle.) On the second try he commented: "You need two lines and a mouth." He followed the same procedure as before and created a similar arrangement (Figure 2h). On the third trial he declared: "I can make it with a fat mouth." Again Eyal adopted the same procedure, drawing two long vertical lines and a connecting horizontal one; this time, however, he added the circle-mouth at the open side of the rectangle. Inspecting the finished product he became confused: the drawing didn't look quite right. Asked to explain his work, he began to romance: "These [vertical lines] are the legs. The [horizontal] line is to keep them out so they can't go in."

At this early stage of graphic representation the child considers the global figure an adequate structural equivalent of the vastly more complex object. Additions to the basic circular structure in the form of arms, legs, hair, ears, or hat are not essential; they merely "make the picture pretty." The child distinguishes clearly between his own work and that of others. When an adult shows a drawing of a circle with facial features and asks a child to identify it, most likely he will perceive it as the face or head of a man. He does not mistake it for a person. Evidently the child applies different criteria to his own work than to that of others.

The representational concepts embodied in the early models described so far are circularity, facial features, and verticality. A similar development can be found in the three-dimensional medium. In his exploration of the playdough the child passes through several stages such as playing with the dough and including it in his action-games. Eventually he invents more specific motions such as rolling a snake, flattening the dough to a pancake shape, rounding it into balls, and even shaping an erect, standing

Young Children's Sculpture and Drawing

column. To make a visually expressive shape such as a sphere requires concerted and prolonged effort. A snake type formation is easier since it requires only rolling the dough back and forth on the table, while a ball requires a persistent rotating motion.

Modeling the human figure begins with the undifferentiated blob of dough from which crude, nonsymmetrical structures evolve. Three different models emerge as the first representations of the human: the upright standing column; the ball or slab of dough with facial features; and the array of separate parts, consisting mainly of facial features but occasionally including limbs.

The most common model of a man is a lengthened blob of dough, crudely shaped, held in the air or placed erect on the table. It is a primitive upright column with little modeling and the parts of the figure often are designated verbally. Holding up the playdough figure emphasizes its verticality and likeness to the object and circumvents the difficulty of making a standing, well balanced figure. The representational concepts of verticality and erectness seem to determine this model of a man depicted in Figures 4, 5, and 6. (The cracks in the sculptures of Figure 6 resulted from playdough drying.) The rear models of Figure 6 lack facial features; that in the front has eyes.

The following example illustrates the child's working procedure and his attitude to the finished product. Doron (4-0) performed a number of successive actions on his portion of playdough. He first added some more to the bulk of dough, then fingered, pulled, pressed, pinched, and indented it. The resulting product remained crudely shaped, with a bloblike appearance, and the boy designated its "parts" as follows: "This is the head, the nose, the mouth, the hair." On his second try he pressed the dough, lengthened it, then held it up in the air. The

Exploration of Forms

4. *Global upright model of playdough. Top, middle, and bottom parts are designated as head, tummy, and legs respectively (boy 4-4).*

5. *Global vertical models of playdough. Erect standing columnlike figures, with indented facial features and pinched out feet; two figures have arms (boy 6-0).*

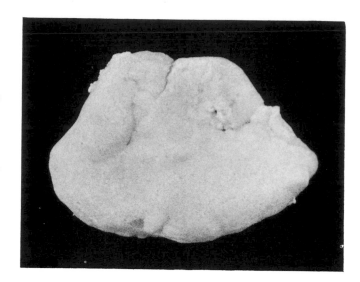

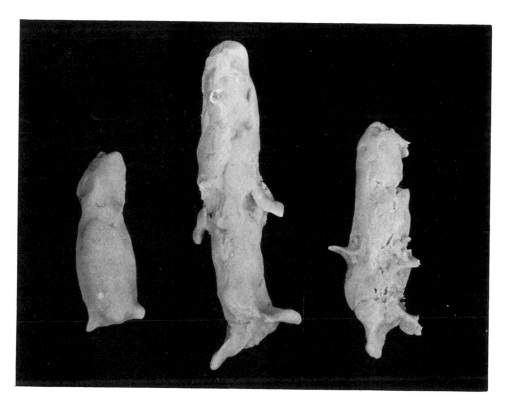

6. Global upright standing vertical figures. Center figure with eyes (boy 3-10); side figures are faceless (boys 3-6 and 4-0).

Exploration of Forms

figure was still crude (see Figure 6, right-hand figure), and Doron designated "head, eyes, tummy, bag." On the third trial he rolled and lengthened the dough, squeezed the top part, and folded his fingers around the rest of the figure, shaping it slightly in the process. Again he held the figure up and designated the top as the head, the middle as the tummy, the lower part as the man's side: "On his side the man carries a bag filled with apples."

As intriguing as the phenomenon of verbal designation is its counterpart—pointing out what the figure is missing. Children declare "he is not going to have," "he doesn't have," "I won't make him," "it's going to be a little man with no face; it's not going to have eyes, mouth, it's just going to have hair."

In earlier stages the child needed primitive prerepresentational devices such as romancing, action-imitation, and reading-off to substitute for representational skill and concept. With his first three-dimensional model of a man he crosses the threshold to representation proper. The figure is still crude and undifferentiated, determined by position and height of the playdough-blob. In order to provide the characteristics of the human figure the child "completes" the sculpture verbally. The designations of parts usually reveal that the child has a clear perceptual concept of what a man looks like, what is the top and what the bottom of the figure. The crude sculpture is interpreted in terms of man's basic visual characteristics. At this early stage there is still a considerable gap between modeling skill and invention of adequate forms. This necessitates reliance on the figure's undifferentiated characteristics. Indeed, the global figure represents a very early step in the modeling of a man.

A distinction should be made between the earlier developmental form of reading-off and designation. In the case of designation the figure is made to

conform to the representational intention despite the
lack of visual similarity. The parts are interpreted
according to some principle such as location on a
vertical axis: top is head, center is tummy, bottom is
legs. Designation requires the notion of
correspondence. The discovery that the top of the
bulky structure is equivalent to the upper part of a
person is a remarkable step and further
representational development depends on it. The
determination to create a specific object and the
ability to sustain this intention while shaping—rather
unsuccessfully—a blob of dough is a significant
achievement. It also reveals the capacity to
subordinate the modeling actions, looks of the figure,
and verbalization of parts to a central, dominant
representational intention.

Another frequently employed model is a ball or
flattened blob of playdough. The facial features are
scratched on its surface, poked out, or separately
formed and attached to the global structure. Although
this figure lacks the determinants of verticality and
upright posture, it makes up for them through
modeling of facial features. The facial features seem
to provide the distinct characteristics of the human
figure. The child also makes use of ready blemishes
in the dough, which can be interpreted according to
their location. He lets the global form represent the
face as well as the entire body. This is illustrated
in Figures 7, 8, and 9. Occasionally all the major parts
of the human body are inscribed on a slab of
playdough as in Figure 10. With its eyes, nose, mouth,
tummy, and legs, this figure bears a striking
resemblance to the drawings which differentiate the
parts of the body inside the drawn contour. It is a
graphic model imposed on a three-dimensional
medium.

Occasionally the child models a sphere and,
without adding facial features, declares it to be a man

Exploration of Forms

or a doll. Anath (3-8) took a lumpy, bulky piece of dough, stroked it, handled it lightly, and placed small unshaped pieces of dough on the surface of the blob: "I take a bit and put it here, eyes, nose, and now the mouth." According to her, this is a "whole mummy," head and body (see Figure 8). Micah (4-2): "I have to do the best I can, so you have to let me do anything I want. Now—I make two little dots to make the eyes. His mouth is open 'cause he is eating. O.K., that's the best I can do." His figure consisted of a bulky, somewhat flattened, global form, with eyes formed separately and placed on the surface and mouth a crack in the dough. Irith (3-9) rolled the dough into a ball. "This is not just the head, it is a

7. Spheric model with facial features (girl 3-10).

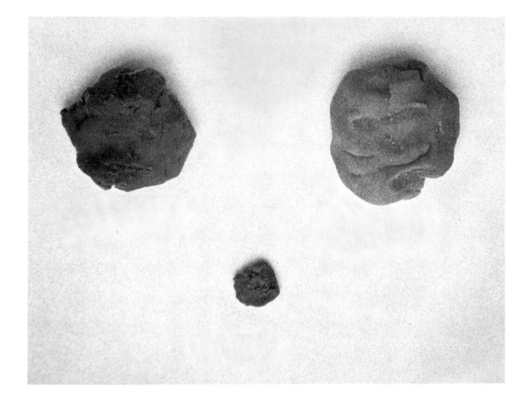

8. *Global model with facial features (girl 3-8).*

9. *Spheric models with facial features; two with legs (boy 4-2).*

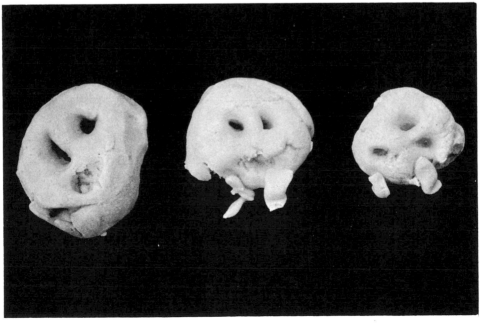

10. Facial features, tummy, and legs are inscribed on the flattened slabs of playdough (girl 5-10).

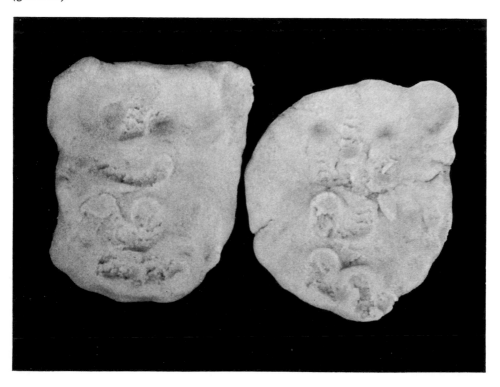

Young Children's Sculpture and Drawing

doll." When asked to make a daddy and a mummy she proceeded in the same fashion, rounding balls of dough and declaring them to be people. Avala (3-10) drew her people as circles and modeled them as spheres.

The third model in playdough is a persistent, though infrequently used, representation of a man. It consists of an arrangement of single facial features. Occasionally arms and legs are also modeled and placed under the facial features. All the parts are formed separately and assembled on the table, without playdough background or contour. Interestingly, the spatial orientation of the parts to each other is rather well preserved. Evidently the surface on which the parts are laid out provides an adequate background and is incorporated implicitly into the representation. For the child this is not a fragmented figure. Such a model, complete with eyes, nose, mouth, tummy, and legs, can be seen in Figure 11. This figure of a man was done by a five-year-old boy with little modeling experience. Younger children make simpler versions of such a layout model as illustrated in Figure 12.

Sara (4-0) illustrates the modeling procedure adopted for this type of figure quite well. She tore several pieces off the lump of dough and flattened them. As she pulled a piece off, she announced the parts she was making: eyes, nose, mouth, legs, feet. All the parts were laid out on the table, much like puzzle pieces, and almost pasted onto the tabletop. When asked to explain the parts of her figure, she identified the two eyes, and named the small center piece "nose" as well as "mouth." Coming to the larger central part she stated that she did not know what it was. The two vertically aligned pieces were legs and feet respectively. She made it clear that her figure was complete: "the whole thing is the body" (Figure 12g).

Exploration of Forms

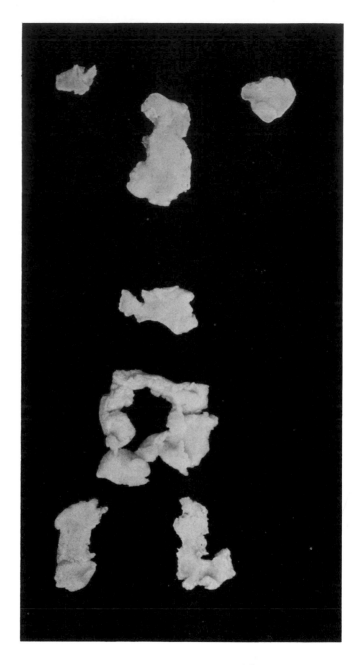

11. Layout model. Facial features, tummy, and legs are formed separately and detached (girl 5-4).

12. Variations of the layout model. Facial features are separately formed and arranged on table top; head contours are missing (children 2-4 to 4-7); artist's sketch; facing page.

Young Children's Sculpture and Drawing

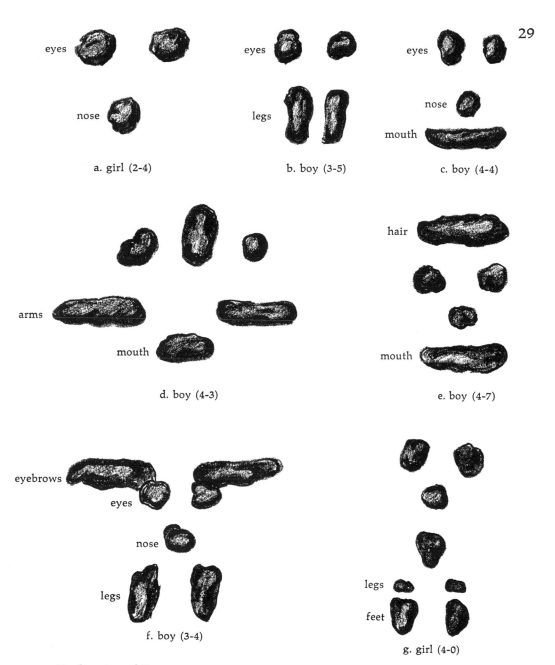

a. girl (2-4)

b. boy (3-5)

c. boy (4-4)

d. boy (4-3)

e. boy (4-7)

f. boy (3-4)

g. girl (4-0)

Exploration of Forms

From the early sculpting models we can infer the concepts which gave rise to them. Like those of drawings, the concepts are characterized by generality —a global form can stand for another global entity, in this case a person. Verticality, uprightness, and facial features also serve as defining attributes of the human figure.

The representation of the human figure in the two media reveals similarities as well as differences. In both media the earliest representations are global figures. In modeling, solutions particularly suited to the medium are devised—such as the upright standing column which lacks facial features and elicits them verbally; in drawings, the circle is filled with the facial features and does not seem to require verbal explanation. Instead, graphically nondistinct parts such as the trunk are implicitly included within the confines of the circle. The implicit inclusion of parts in drawing may be akin to the verbal designation of the sculptures. In general, the two-dimensional medium elicits more depiction of detail and embellishment: the big circle requires something additional, and marks are made with relative ease. In modeling there is less emphasis on detail; this will be so even when the figure develops, differentiates, and becomes a fully articulate representation of a man. In both media we find the model consisting of a basic unit with prominent facial features. In modeling as well as in drawing this represents the *whole* man, and the explicit characterization of the facial features makes the global unit an expressive representation of the human figure. This similarity extends to the single representation of features, which appears in modeling as well as in drawing, although this model is used infrequently and is quickly improved.

Genuine three-dimensional treatment of the figure is rare at this stage. An exception is the work of a

boy (3-10) who made a global man with facial
features, turned the figure over and said: "Now his
back on—that's all done."

We have seen how difficult the evolution of forms
and models can be. Many youngsters complain that
the task is too hard, that they can't do it yet, that they
are not old enough; and some refuse outright. To
be faced with an amorphous task can be very
frustrating. In such an unstructured and bewildering
situation, a mere question addressed to the child may
provide a starting point, a spark to be pursued. For
example, Rachel (3-10) was asked to model a person.
After a good deal of hesitation on her part, and
encouraging remarks on the part of the examiner, she
took the lump of dough: "I want to make a small
ball and a big ball. I like to make lots of balls . . .
also a snake . . . now I shall do—I know how to make
a bracelet." Meanwhile she rolled the dough between
her hands, lengthened it, and held it up. She did not
perform any work on the table. In the process of
rolling the dough back and forth she gained some
familiarity with it, pulling, lengthening, and shaping
it. The examiner reminded her that she was supposed
to make a person, coaxed, and promised a present.
Rachel: "How do you go about it? I don't know."
Experimenter: "What does a mummy have?"
Rachel: "Eyes!" This provided an inspiration. She
scratched two eyes on the surface of the piece of
dough; next she slapped the dough on the table,
pounded it, and explained: "That's a face." She
flattened it some more and clearly inscribed eyes in
the slab of dough. "That's the daddy; he has eyes and
a nose and a mouth. He has no legs." Rachel
deliberately "drew" the features on the flattened
surface.

Children strive to attain visual likeness to the
object; and failing this, they frequently criticize their
work. A recurrent complaint is that the drawing does

Exploration of Forms

not look like a person. Thus, children attempt to establish a better correspondence between their representation and the object by "renaming." A little girl (3-7), who had set out to draw her father, drew an oval head-body with lines and stated with surprise: "Daddy is now Humpty-Dumpty!" (Figure 13).

At every step the child's representational intention outstrips his ability to draw and model. He may describe in detail the kind of person he is going to make, reveal fine and accurate observation of the object, yet produce a simple global figure. He tends to represent in a minimal fashion, and if he succeeds in creating a general likeness to the object he is satisfied. Statements such as "it needs feet, but I won't make them," "he is too lazy to put on his tie," "I'll make a person with no eyes" abound. At this stage the child attempts to create with the utmost economy of means. Representation is hard work and drawing or modeling can be an exhausting effort,

13. Daddy is now Humpty-Dumpty (girl 3-7); artist's sketch.

Young Children's Sculpture and Drawing

which leaves the three-year-old, after a few trials, utterly fatigued.

Although early representations of a man have many characteristics in common, variations on the human theme are, even at this stage, manifold, and reveal the inventiveness of the young artists.

The evolution from the scribble and playdough action to the first articulate forms represents a milestone in the child's development and reveals dramatic progress in his capacity for symbolic processes. Within the span of a few months, moving from scribbles to the primordial man, the child creates order and beauty where scribble-chaos once prevailed. He learns to control whirls and zigzags and subdues them in his quest to depict something, usually a person or an animal. In order to appreciate this accomplishment, let us reconsider the difficulties the child encountered on his way to representation.

The task of modeling or drawing a human is a particularly difficult one. Unlike building blocks or puzzle pieces, which the child can use very efficiently at this age, paper and playdough are totally unstructured materials, and the request to make a person is equally ambiguous. This instruction does not contain much useful information: it does not specify what kind of a man to make, what parts to include, and above all how to differentiate them graphically or plastically. It is up to the child to define the task to himself, to invent the forms, and to identify them. The child who draws a circle has to decide whether it will stand for the head, the entire person, or perhaps the neck. This is not a simple case of similarity; mere recognition will not suffice, since a man does not consist of lines and circles. It is the child who creates the *equivalence* between a form—a line on paper or a blob of dough—and a realistic object. By inventing forms and symbolizing them they become truly representative.

Exploration of Forms

Simultaneously, the child must order these forms and create an acceptable part-whole relationship. This is the case when he adds facial features inside the circle-contour. In the process he has discovered one- and two-dimensional use of lines, and he has learned to utilize space. The paper serves not only as background for delineation, but also as a medium. Together with the lines it contributes to the creation of form and figure. In addition to the demanding requirements of defining the task, creating the forms, and imparting meaning and organization to the picture, the child has to master the perceptual coordination of complex motor skills. He has started literally from scratch and produced a recognizable form.

The difficulties of mastering a three-dimensional medium are not unlike those encountered in drawing. Playdough is unstructured material; mere handling of it creates very few new forms, and less expressive ones than crayon-on-paper. Most youngsters have little experience with playdough for modeling purposes. In American nursery schools playdough is provided to make "cookies." The children are used to flatten the dough and to cut it into cookie shapes. Some schools provide special rollers. Thus the action on the playdough is perhaps of an imitational nature, like mother rolling the dough, flattening it, cutting and shaping the cookies, making birthday cakes, and the like. Playdough is usually not available in Israeli nursery schools, but plasticene is freely supplied. The latter seems not to be associated with baking, and there is less flattening of the material. Occasionally spontaneous modeling attempts are seen among the three-year-olds, such as rolling a snake or a bracelet, or making a basket or Sabbath candles. Many youngsters, however, when confronted with an outright "representational" task feel quite helpless and complain that it is too hard and that they can't do it.

The passage from a prerepresentational attitude to the first attempts at modeling a human involves a radical transformation in outlook and competence. Sammy (2-10), a friendly prenursery schooler, was given a portion of playdough and asked to make a ball. He smiled at the examiner, hit the dough lightly on the table, turned it in his hand, and waited for further instruction. When asked to make a cup, and then a doll, he continued to smile and to turn the dough aimlessly in his hand. Evidently the instruction contained no information that he could use. He did not quite comprehend what he was supposed to do and reverted to pounding the dough lightly on the table, saying: "I want to learn, I don't know."

A profound distance exists between this child and the one who makes a crude column-blob with designated parts. It is this distance which the prerepresentational child masters in the course of a few months, provided he is given the chance to explore the medium freely.

3 Growth and Differentiation: The Tadpole Man

Transformation of the primordial one-unit figure, composed of the large circle with facial features, heralds a new phase in representational development. The first human model is a global figure, and graphic differentiation of parts and features is confined *inside* the circle. We now witness the transition of this primitive figure to an oval-shaped oblong with the face drawn in the upper part and two verticals extending *outside* the contours, as illustrated in Figures 14, 15, and 16. This charming but peculiar looking man has been called "tadpole man," "homme têtard," or "Kopffüssler." Some older investigators interpreted these drawings as subsuming the body within the large contour (Sully, 1896, 1910). Later writers misinterpreted them as "syncretistic" creations, as confused and incomplete representations of a man (Luquet, 1913; Werner, 1948; Piaget, 1926, 1951, 1969). According to this view, the child's incapacity to analyze a figure and organize components doomed him to juxtapose parts or omit them altogether. Another principle explained his selection of the parts drawn: presumably the child drew what was most important to him—the head—and simply forgot the rest.

More recently, the nonpictorial and structural origins of the tadpole figures have been stressed (Kellogg, 1959, 1969). This interpretation considers the tadpole man an outgrowth of the mandala- and sun- schemata, which are determined primarily by the brain's preference for ordered and balanced structures; thus, form dominates over pictorial quality and according to this view the figure should not be assessed in terms of its likeness to the object. Careful observation, however, reveals that the large circular contour comprises the head as well as the body (Arnheim, 1954; Golomb, 1969, 1973). The child illustrates this when he draws the face in the upper part of the circle and the body in its center

14. *Tadpole figures*
(girl 3-9, boy 4-0).

15. *More tadpole figures*
(boys 3-6 and 4-7).

Young Children's Sculpture and Drawing

(Figure 3). His explanations make it abundantly clear that the body has not been forgotten but usually is located in the center part of the circle. The need for graphic depiction of this part has not yet been recognized.

Gradually the primordial circle shrinks and the vertical lines lengthen. The circle now becomes the exclusive domain of head and face, and the body "descends" between the two vertical lines. The verticals serve a dual function; representing the body's outline as well as the legs. Children are quite ingenious in depicting the tummy as a scribble (Figures 17 and 18a), bellybutton (Figure 18b), or a circle inside the new boundaries (Figure 18c). Occasionally the child draws the verticals to indicate the body's contour, and extends them further to represent the legs (Figure 18d). Sammy (4-7) drew a big circle and two vertical lines under it. He seemed to consider what to do next—"I think what to put inside the doll"—and promptly drew a circle between the verticals to represent the tummy (Figure 18e).

16. Elaborate tadpole figures (girl 4-4).

Growth and Differentiation

17. Tadpole figure.
Scribble between the
two vertical extensions
denotes trunk (boy 4-7).

Frequently, in response to a question about his drawing, the presence of the tummy is verbally designated, as the child points to the space between the verticals as the place for it. The area within the two parallel lines does not strike the child as "empty" space but is perceived as part of the figure. When children are presented with a graphically incomplete figure consisting of head, legs, and arms, the majority considers it a complete picture of a man and locates the tummy between the two vertical lines. The same results can be obtained when the figure is presented for graphic completion of parts (see Chapter 6).

Occasionally head and body are drawn in a disjointed manner. This might be related to the paper-as-medium. The paper is a medium for markings, and as such provides continuity for the parts. The open space does not yet "separate" the parts from each other. Only when the child discovers that attached forms and separate contours "look better," do detached forms look like segregated or free floating parts. Only at this point does the need for bounding lines and separate contours arise.

18. Early efforts to depict the trunk (children 3-9 to 5-2); artist's sketch.

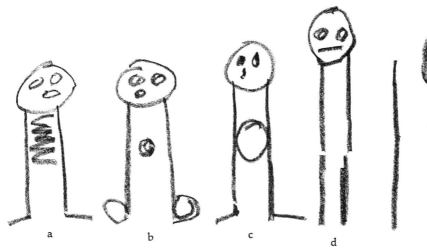

a   b   c   d   e

Growth and Differentiation

The placement of the arms varies with the size of the circle and the sequence of drawn parts. When the circle is large and the legs short, the arms are usually drawn from the circle. When the circle shrinks and the legs lengthen, the placing of the arms often depends on the sequence in which the several parts are drawn. If the verticals precede the drawing of the arms, the latter are usually extended from the verticals; if the arms precede the drawing of the legs they usually extend from the circle.

At this stage of development the predominant graphic model of a human is the tadpole figure. Several examples are shown in Figures 19 and 20.

19. Variations on the tadpole theme (children 3-6 to 5-1).

Young Children's Sculpture and Drawing

20. Further variations on the tadpole theme (children 3-5 to 5-5); artist's sketch.

Two other graphic models, the linear and the contourless man, continue to be explored in several variations. The linear model, which emphasizes verticality at the expense of head or face, is quite prevalent. Stick-figures can also be subsumed under this model. Figures 21, 22, 23, and 24 illustrate the linear model of a man. Some children omit the body contour altogether (see Figures 25 and 26).

The "tadpoles," and contourless models of Figures 17 to 26 are a sample of the seemingly inexhaustible variety of forms which children produce on this basic theme. No tadpole is truly like any other, and a great deal of exploration and variation of form can be found in the drawings of an individual child. Figure 27 shows a family consisting of father, mother, and daughter. The father (middle) is an example of the "open" trunk. The head is graphically differentiated

Young Children's Sculpture and Drawing

from the body, but the body-contour is incomplete, that is, an example of a graphically ambiguous or indistinct form. This drawing is somewhat more advanced than the tadpole figure with arms extending from the circle. The human with the "open" trunk represents a typical graphic model, frequently employed; in the developmental progression it follows the tadpole man with long verticals. The mother (left) is represented by an outline which encompasses head and body; the facial features are drawn in the upper section, with tummy and the bellybutton placed in the center. Hair and hands extend from the contour, while legs and feet are graphically well differentiated. The graphic model employed for the daughter is very similar to that of the mother, although the contour is incomplete and the hair is adorned with a ribbon.

21. Linear tadpole figures (children 3-6 to 5-5); artist's sketch.

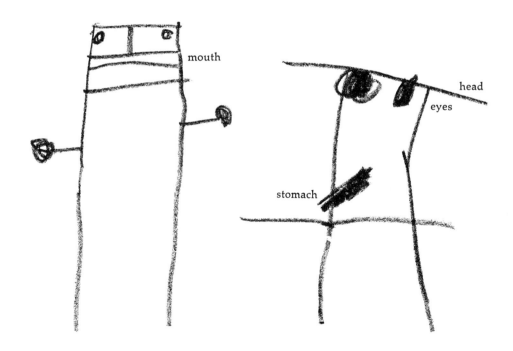

22. *Tadpole figures emphasizing the body's vertical dimension (girls 3-4 and 3-9).*

23. *Elongated tadpole figures (boy 4-2, girl 4-2).*

Young Children's Sculpture and Drawing

DADDY

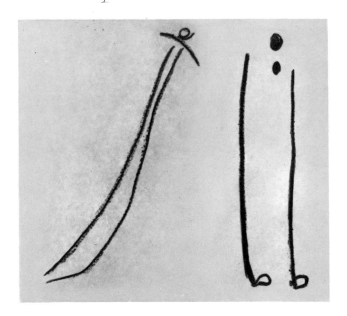

24. Linear figures emphasizing the length of the human body (children 4-6, 5-1 and 5-2).

25. Figure with contourless trunk (girl 4-0).

26. Figures without head or body contours (children 3-9 to 5-3); artist's sketch.

Young Children's Sculpture and Drawing

Growth and Differentiation

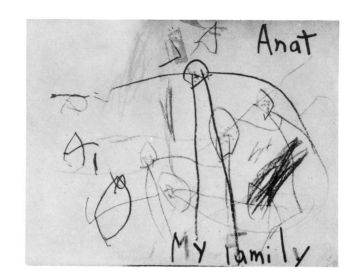

28. *My family (girl 3-9).*

29. *Children (girl 3-10).*

Figures 28, 29, and 30, by two three-year-old girls (sisters), were drawn during the free play period in nursery school. Unlike requested drawings, made one at a time on separate sheets of paper, they teem with people and give us an inkling of the feeling for composition and of aesthetic delight manifested by these youngsters.

30. My family (girl 3-6).

Growth and Differentiation

Since this study was concerned with the growth of form, the use of crayon or pencil seemed adequate for drawing. The true delight in children's art work for both viewer and artist, however, derives from the child's freedom to use several colors in a drawing, and employ various tools such as magic markers, paint and brushes, fingers and sponges. Depending on whether crayon, pencil, or magic marker is used, the ease of drawing varies; the size of the figure may also be affected by the choice of either pencil or magic marker. Compared with the magic marker or brush, the crayon is somewhat constraining, demanding greater effort on the part of the three- or four-year-old. The choice of several colors does not seem to affect form qua form; the child indicates that the different colors make his picture "pretty."

Experimentation with graphic forms can lead to spontaneous discoveries and to dramatic improvement of the graphic model in a few tries. Judy (4-0) drew a large elliptical shape, added a neck on top, followed by a head. Inspecting it, she remarked: "There is the head and the throat and a big snowball." Her second drawing consisted of a large circular shaped head-body, eyes, mouth, tongue, arms, legs, and feet. Though the second drawing does not include a graphically distinct trunk, it presents a more articulate representation of a human than the first drawing (Figure 31a).

Jimmy (4-5) made two drawings of a person. The first consisted of two eyes, a mouth, two arms, two legs, and two ears, but lacked an outline for the facial features; Jimmy named it "a person monster." On the second trial he drew the facial features followed by the enclosing outline, commenting "That face goes around it." He completed his picture by adding hair and legs (Figure 31b).

When the head of the tadpole man is too small to contain the eyes, the child draws them in part inside and in part outside the circle-head. This happened

Young Children's Sculpture and Drawing

to Gay (3-9) on her first attempt. Spontaneously
she started a second drawing, enlarging the head so
the two eyes could well fit into the circle-head. These
quite spontaneous corrections reveal the young
artist's need for articulation and improvement of
forms. At times, the eyes are drawn too large and
the mouth has to move outside the circle, under the
head. Hila (3-9) drew several pictures of a person.
Each time the mouth was placed under the head,
since the space inside the circle already was taken up
by the eyes. The successive drawings show
spontaneous improvement in the cohesion of the
parts. On the fourth try she was instructed to draw a
man with a "big head." Accordingly, Hila drew a
large oval, placed the eyes and the mouth *inside* the
circle, and extended the limbs from the inside of the
contour to the outside. Evidently, the large circle
provoked a more primitive representation of the
human figure (Figure 31c).

The first drawing of Narkis (3-6) consisted of a
concentric spiral-like form which she called a "kite."
Her second consisted of four long parallel lines,
drawn diagonally across the paper, with a small circle
at its top. Heavy horizontally drawn lines filled the
area between the circle and the diagonals. The circle
represented head and eye; the lines, body and legs;
and the crissscross scribble, the throat. On her third
trial she started with a circle (head and eye), followed
by three parallel lines (legs and body). The curved
line between circle and verticals was drawn last and
represented a "blouse." The fourth and last drawing
is an improved version of the first drawing of a
man; head and neck are attached and the body
consists of two verticals. From the first drawing
(kite) to the fourth drawing there is a tremendous
progress, from a nonfigurative design (interpreted in
a pseudo-representational manner) to a somewhat
cluttered representation of a human and finally to the
well-structured figure of the last drawing (Figure 31d).

Growth and Differentiation

a

c

d

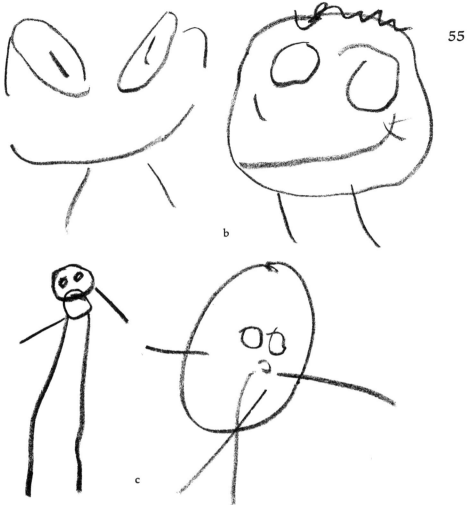

b

c

31. Graphic inventions and spontaneous improvements in the representation of the human figure over several trials (children 3-6 to 4-5); artist's sketch.

Growth and Differentiation

32. *Experimentation with forms over several trials leads to the drawing of graphically differentiated figures (children 3-5 to 4-8); artist's sketch.*

Figure 32 illustrates successive attempts to draw a person. The drawings were done within a single testing session and show spontaneous attempts to differentiate forms and improve graphic articulation. Within the limited span of a few trials these children moved from global representation of a man to the tadpole model—and even beyond.

Young Children's Sculpture and Drawing

b

d

e

Growth and Differentiation

One little girl, Sar (3-8), progressed in a single session from nonrepresentational forms to a graphically differentiated figure. Her first attempt resulted in a pear-shaped oblong, covering almost the entire page. On the second and third tries she produced very similarly shaped figures. She became involved in the task, asked for more paper, and again produced a version similar to the first three drawings. This time, however, she gave it a name: "a turkey." She continued to draw and produced an elongated triangular shape, extending it to the top of the page; this she called "a ghost." Next she turned the paper sideways and drew a complete figure of a person, consisting of head, facial features, tummy, legs, arms, fingers, feet, and toes; this figure was called "a man." The next two, consisting of head, facial features, legs, feet, and toes, are drawings of her "brother." She ended her series with a small picture,

33. Evolution of the human figure in a single testing session (girl 3-8).

"myself as a baby," composed only of head, facial features, and legs (Figure 33). Though exhausted from the intense effort, Sar was immensely pleased with her accomplishment. To witness such a moment of creative invention is a true privilege and elicits in the observer a sense of exhilaration and shared adventure.

The discrepancy between the verbal description of the object and the relatively simple drawing is a rather striking finding. The running commentary accompanying many drawings is more detailed and accurate than the graphic account. A child may describe in detail the kind of person he is going to draw, yet create a simple tadpole man. The following examples illustrate this discrepancy and emphasize the child's effort to interpret, explain, and complete the figure which falls short of his representational intentions. Jen (3-10): "A daddy this time, is going to be looking up. Has cheeks, chin, big body is in towel, pulling it [towel] up . . . big hand and weensie hand is sticking out. Legs and feet are in the towel." Gi (4-0): "I'm going to draw a Santa Claus. Here are the reindeer and the sled. He is supposed to have a hood. How about *you* making an eye for me?" Ed (4-11): "My mummy has a wriggly face—it is hard to make —and long curly hair . . . that's her walking, dancing." Al (4-4) described her finished product: "My mommy . . . her eyes are funny, her hair is in her mouth . . . I forgot the knees, but that's all right." Jennifer (3-10): "The legs will be long, because it is a real big daddy . . . there is the shirt . . . you know daddies wear shirts and pants. Sometimes I do too."

Children do not strive to represent all they know; they are satisfied when the drawing "looks like it." Here is an example of a four-year-old girl who drew all the parts she needed. Gay (4-4): "That's for the legs; I can't make them straight. I can only make the legs, can't make the whole thing . . . I can make the

Growth and Differentiation

60

head too, and the hair. I'll make a picture of her wearing her earrings and a necklace. But I can't make them beautiful. Now the neck so I can put the necklace on it."

Evidently the problem of "complete" representation of the human figure should be viewed as a problem of the *graphic* differentiation of parts. What seems to be a "graphically" incomplete rendition of a figure should not be misconstrued as a simple, direct expression of the child's incomplete and therefore immature concept of a man. The extensive narratives accompanying the drawing reveal that the child is not interested in a complete depiction of what he knows about a man. Much is left out because it is difficult to represent, superfluous to the basic structure of the human, and can be accomplished by verbal description. When he is drawing the young child considers a global likeness sufficient until adequate practice and incidental discoveries lead to the addition of lines to indicate separate body parts and result in a better likeness to the object. The child does not feel compelled to represent all he knows and remembers. A certain playfulness characterizes his attitude toward his own drawing. He may draw someone with two noses, his head floating away, and equip him with extra legs "like an octopus," or he may draw an armless person, decide to give him a pocketbook, and add an arm to carry it.

When the drawings fail to meet the child's standard of likeness, he may criticize his work or offer suitable reinterpretations. Al (3-5): "Is this a man? No, it is an arm. What do you think it looks like? Hat! Don't you think it's sort of crooked? Think it looks like a foot? Looks like umbrella" (Figure 34).

Children are well aware of unusual features in their drawings, and many qualify their drawings as "silly man," "funny man," "Bozo person." Often these youngsters express dissatisfaction with their

34. *Drawing of a man (girl 3-5).*

Young Children's Sculpture and Drawing

drawings but do not attempt to modify or "correct" them. Ray (3-10): "I made only one eye; no room for the other." James (5-4) drew a tadpole figure with arms extending from the big cirle: "Never seen hands coming from the head," he remarked, but left the drawing unchanged. Steve (4-9) drew a person and on inspection renamed it a "bunny."

Thus, children make factual statements about their work and criticize, rename, or reinterpret drawings—"his head is chopped off," "he broke his leg," "comes from the hospital"—but do not attempt to modify them by graphic means. They seem to resign themselves to the odd features. Reinterpretation of the drawing effectively circumvents the need for corrective action and brings, via verbal means, representation and intention into line. The child's position is adaptive rather than corrective.

At this stage of development most youngsters are still indifferent to the relative size of their figures. The first circles are quite large and the other parts, of necessity, are smaller or even squeezed in to fit the limits of the page. The sweeping motion which creates the large circle does not carry a specific emotional or projective significance. Occasionally a youngster may draw a large line for the daddy and a smaller one for the baby, but genuine concern for size differences appears only with further graphic differentiation of the figure. With the evolution of more varied representational forms, the youngster also adopts more stringent requirements for his drawn figure. Sometime, between the ages of four and a half and six he begins to demand better graphic articulation, pays some attention to size differences, and makes the first distinction between male and female figures in terms of hair and clothing.

Altogether the drawing task involves a great deal of effort on the part of the child. Often his whole body is engaged in the motor act, and after a few attempts the youngster may become fatigued. This may well be an additional factor codetermining the young child's tendency to represent with utmost economy of means. By comparison, the older, more experienced youngster creates the main outlines of the figure with relative ease and is eager to go beyond the simple configuration.

In modeling, as in drawing, the tadpole man now gains prominence. In the three-dimensional medium this figure consists of a sphere and legs. The two other sculpting models—the upright standing column and the single features layout model encountered as the very first and embryonic representations of the human figure—persist and are further developed. Three different models can be distinguished at this stage: the tadpole man; the one-unit figure with internal subdivision of its parts; and the graphic model.

Three-dimensional variations on the tadpole theme range from the large disk or sphere with short extensions for legs to the smaller disk with longer legs (Figure 35).

Figures 36, 37, 38, 39, and 41 illustrate the variations in the treatment of the two basic parts of the tadpole man. At times we can follow the development of a tadpole figure from a global to a more differentiated tadpole representation in a single session, over three trials. In Figure 40 the first tadpole consists of an oblong head-body and relatively short legs. In the next two figures the child shrinks the basal unit and lengthens the legs as proper outline for the body. This development is quite similar to that observed in the drawn tadpoles. The majority of the tadpole figures are placed horizontally on the table, but approximately one-third of them are held up or placed in an erect standing posture on the table. Figure 40 shows two erect standing tadpole men.

Young Children's Sculpture and Drawing

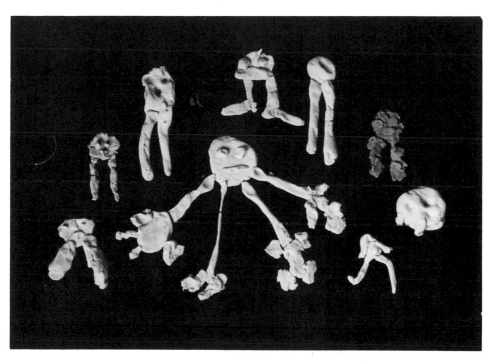

35. Tadpole models of playdough (children 3-4 to 5-0).

Growth and Differentiation

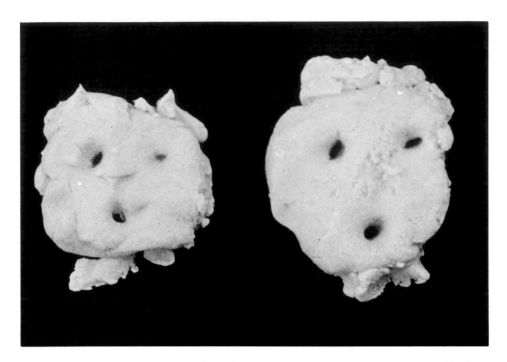

36. Tadpole models.
Figures consist of a
global body with facial
features, tiny legs,
and hair (boy 4-6).

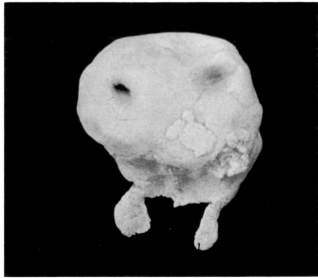

37. Tadpole model with
global body, facial
features, and short legs
(boy 4-8).

Young Children's Sculpture and Drawing

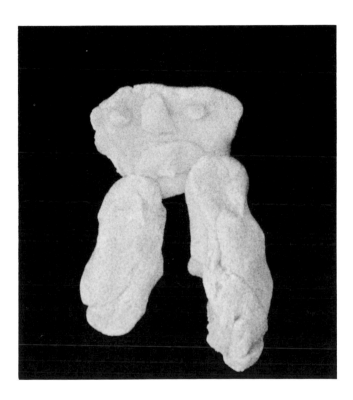

38. Tadpole model with head, facial features, and elongated legs; the legs also represent the body's contour (boy 4-4).

Growth and Differentiation

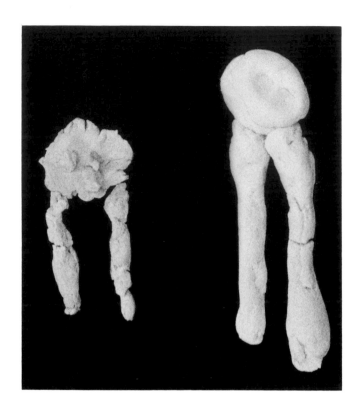

39. Further tadpole models with head, facial features, and elongated legs; the legs also indicate body contour (boys 4-2 and 5-0).

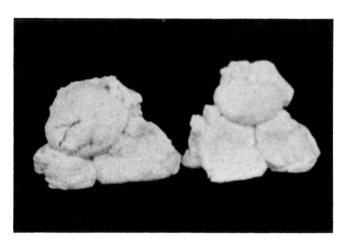

40. Two erect standing tadpole models (boy 5-2).

Young Children's Sculpture and Drawing

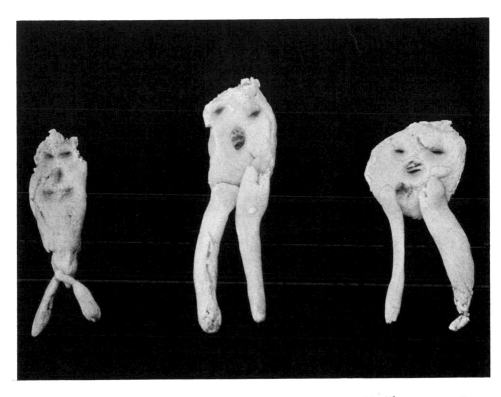

41. *Three consecutive tadpole models. The global oblong (left), modeled first, represents both head and body; the short extensions indicate legs. As the global unit shrinks (center and right), the extensions lengthen and indicate legs as body contour (boy 4-10).*

Growth and Differentiation

The global head-body structure of the tadpole man usually varies from a sphere to a bulky but flattened piece of dough or a disk-shaped unit. A common working procedure consists of rolling the dough into a ball, flattening it with the palm of the hand, then adding separate pieces for the legs. These may be rolled like sausages and attached to the global structure or put together in a piecemeal fashion (Figure 42, top). Some children paste tiny pieces together to make the legs and hair. In American nursery schools children frequently comment "Gotta make it flat," as though they meant to say: got to make it flat like paper. Unless it is flattened, the dough medium seems unworkable to those children. Among Israeli children such comments were exceedingly rare, and the percentage of upright standing tadpoles was higher than that of their American counterparts.

Once the dough-form has been flattened, the facial features are scratched in, poked out, or separately formed and attached so that the features are raised. At times they are placed on the surface of the disk and pressed into the dough until they almost disappear in in the soft background. Alene (3-6) first rolled the dough into a ball and then pressed it slightly into an ovalish shape. Next she rolled two longish strips of dough into sausages and attached them to the "head." While working she held the growing figure up, supported the head with her hand, and left the appendages dangling. A crack in the head was interpreted as a tooth, the appendages were conceived as legs containing the tummy in between. Since the figure was held up, the child achieved a vertical posture without having to balance an upright standing figure.

Gina (4-0) made a flat, circular shaped piece and placed tiny bits of pink playdough on it. "I'm putting pink eyes on, little teeny tiny eyes; you can't see very

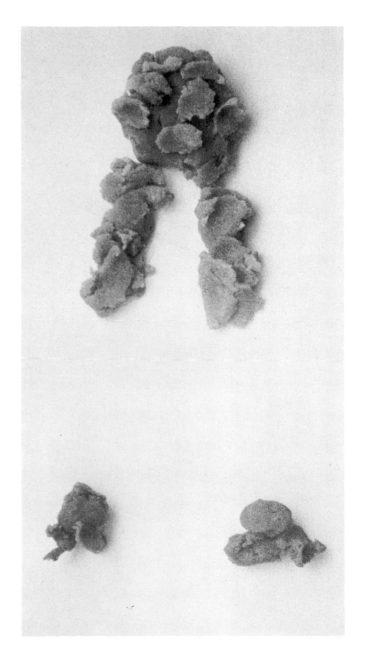

42. *Different sized tadpoles (girls 3-6 and 3-9).*

Growth and Differentiation

well with tiny eyes. This is all I'm gonna make, I'll finish another time . . . have to make the legs." She rolled two snakes for legs, and attached them while holding the figure up in a vertical posture. "One of legs is short cause he was shot." This interpretation is offered as an on-the-spot justification for the lack of symmetry she observed.

Arbel's (3-9) first action was to flatten a large piece of dough with the palm of her hand. She subsequently pulled small pieces off it and placed the essentially unformed parts on the flattened surface to represent eyes, mouth, and cheeks. Two slightly elongated strips became eyebrows. The legs were pieced together, bit by bit (Figure 42 top). The treatment of the facial features recalls the drawing of these parts. Instead of the simple and visually clear line to represent the legs and body-outline, the legs are created by pasting unformed parts together. Thus, an essentially graphic model of a tadpole man has been modified by the medium properties of the playdough.

Aby (5-2) planned his man as an upright standing figure. Accordingly, he started with the legs; he held two lumpy bits of dough up and then placed them on the table. Next he rolled and rounded some dough into a ball and placed it on top of the legs: "Now the head . . . little eyes . . . I don't have to make the nose, no space for the nose." His second figure was constructed similarly: the legs were placed on the table and the head attached to the upright standing legs. Unworked pieces of dough served as facial features. Both figures stood on the table (Figure 41), but Aby complained that the structure was unstable.

The upright standing column encountered earlier, now develops into a figure consisting of a basic unit with some internal subdivision representing individual parts. The head is usually pulled out or shaped by pressing the fingers around the top section; arms and legs are pinched out; and the facial features are represented in a minimal fashion. At this stage of modeling a figure the child need no longer rely on verbal designation of parts or on mere verticality to create likeness to the object. Inspection of Figures 43, 44, 45, 46, and 47 reveals crudely modeled sculptures whose facial features have been omitted or marked sloppily. With the exception of the symmetrical and upright standing column there is no observable effort at precise workmanship, and the details of the figure are barely indicated.

The majority of these one-unit models are erect, standing sculptures, though occasionally a flattened and horizontally placed one-unit model is found, as in Figures 46 and 47. The procedure adopted for the flattened model is exemplified by Yoram (5-5), who worked the whole blob of dough in his hand, subdividing the figure by pulling the head and the limbs out of the bulk of dough. He then placed the figure on the table and flattened the "stomach" with his fist. Three indentations in the face created eyes and nose. The overall workmanship is crude, yet the figure does not require verbal designation since its several parts have been modeled (Figure 46).

A variation on the one-unit figure can be seen in sculptures consisting of a column and a head or a global body with a separately formed head attached to it, such as Figure 48.

The graphic model in playdough is an interesting line of development in this medium. We previously encountered the layout of single features as one of the earliest representational models of a man. This model might be considered a precursor of the "graphic" model in sculpting. Essentially it is a linear model which evolves from the representation of features and parts, borrows concepts and procedures from drawing, and may eventually become quite perfected. Unlike the typical modeling procedures already

Growth and Differentiation

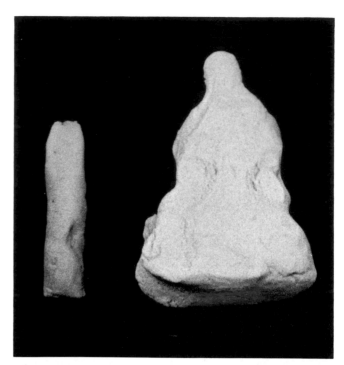

43. *Erect one-unit models (boys 4-0 and 4-7).*

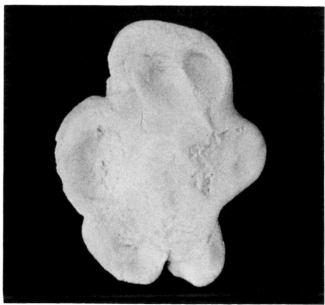

44. *Another erect one-unit model (girl 3-9).*

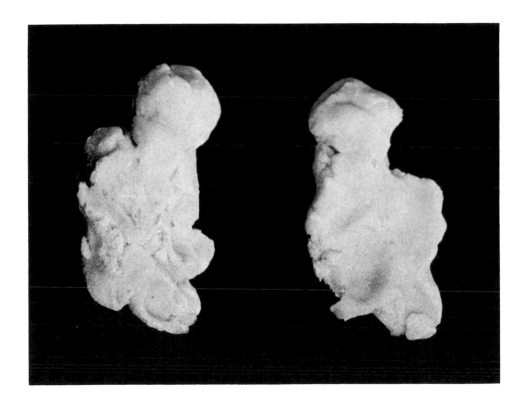

*45. Erect one-unit
models, continued
(girl 5-3).*

Growth and Differentiation

74

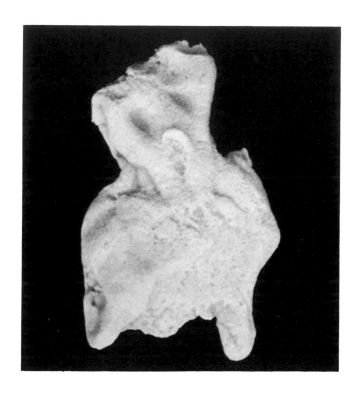

46. *Flattened horizontal one-unit model (boy 5-5).*

Young Children's Sculpture and Drawing

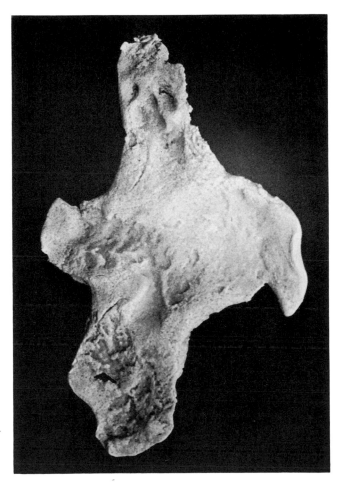

47. *Flattened one-unit model, continued (boy 6-0).*

48. *Erect models with global column-body and head (boy 4-0, girl 3-8).*

49. A graphic tadpole model in playdough (girl 4-4).

described, whereby a figure is constructed from several solid parts or modeled from one piece of dough, the graphic model employs two-dimensional representational concepts and procedures. One gets the impression that the child "draws" the playdough figure—and indeed he does outline head and body contours with thin strips of playdough. Figure 49 exemplifies the transposition of the graphic tadpole model to the three-dimensional medium. Figure 50 illustrates a slightly different version of the graphic model of a tadpole man and offers a glimpse of ongoing processes of differentiation. The figure on the left consists of a flattened but solid head with facial features (eyes, nose, mouth, forehead) and two extensions to represent the body outline; hair has been draped around the head. The figure to the right has been constructed similarly, but shows a clear improvement; the body contour has been completed ("I'll close the doll"), and a bellybutton has been added for further differentiation. Figure 51 modeled by a girl (4-7) is a "pure" sample of the graphic model with both head and body outlines; the facial features and the buttons are placed inside the contours.

50. Further graphic models in playdough; tadpole figure (left), and figure with a bellybutton and outline trunk (right) (girl 5-0).

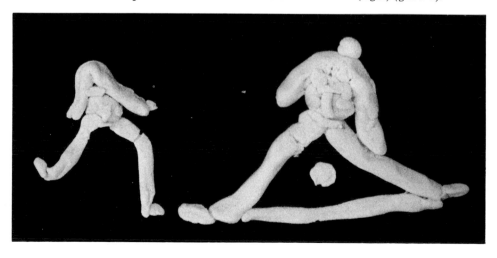

Growth and Differentiation

A variant of the graphic model consists of an orderly array of pieces, some attached and some detached, laid out on the table like a puzzle assembly. Figures 52 and 53 illustrate this model of a man. Figure 53 was made by a girl (3-9) who first prepared the several parts and only then assembled them. Though she adopted a graphic model as illustrated in the "open" trunk typical of the drawn human, the construction of the figure is quite unlike drawing in several respects. In drawing, each part follows the other in a special order, from the top down or vice versa. In this figure, however, the "preparation of parts" seems to follow from the qualities of the three-dimensional medium. With further practice the detached forms are joined together and soon the "puzzle" figure is transformed into a proper graphic model or it evolves into a more conventional sculpture consisting of solid parts.

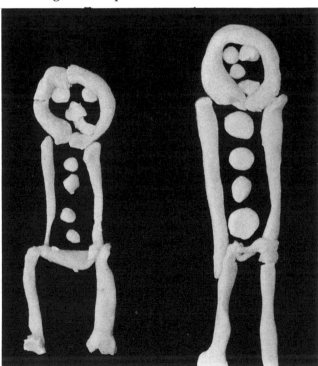

51. Graphic models in playdough; head and body contours are outlined with strips of playdough (girl 4-7).

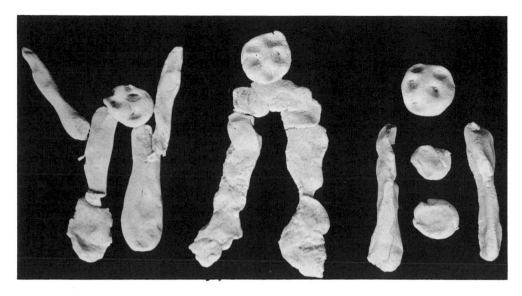

52. Graphic models in playdough; figures with open trunk (boy 6-0).

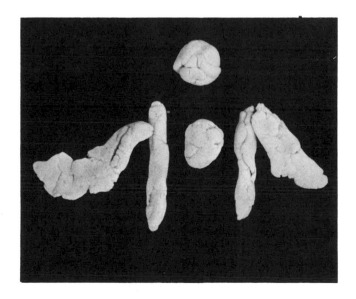

53. Graphic model in playdough; figure with open trunk and tummy (girl 3-9).

Growth and Differentiation

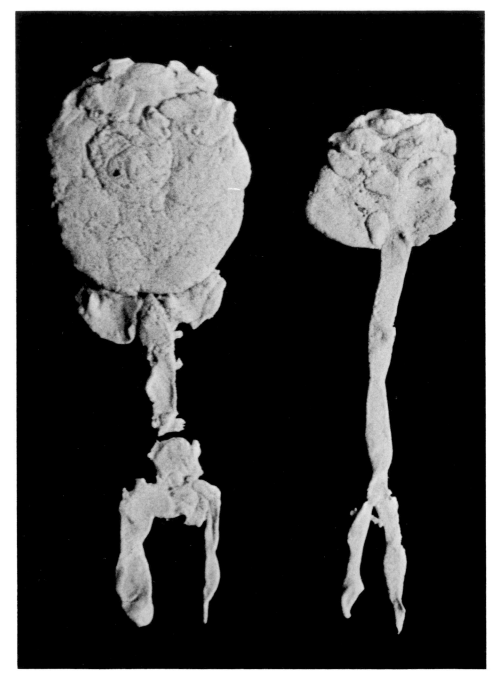

The following finding is intriguing. Children who make a man consisting of an array of single features and detached parts, nevertheless construct a complete and erect standing snowman composed of two to three balls of dough, stacked on top of each other. In Chapter 6 we shall look more closely at the models of snowmen and consider the theoretical implications of the models and their selective application.

The stick-figure in playdough can be considered yet another version of the graphic model and has been described previously as a two-dimensional model. Figures 54, 55, 56, 57, and 58 depict the stick-figure model in the three-dimensional medium. Figure 54 was created in the following manner. Abe (4-7): ". . . don't know . . . O.K. I'll make a man, I'll make a funny head, a dog's head, here is his face, I'll make

54. Stick figures in playdough (boy 4-7); facing page.

55. Stick figures, continued (girl 4-9).

Growth and Differentiation

him eyes, there is the nose, eyebrows . . . here is the mouth, the neck. A doll, a doll, hand for the man, a long neck like a giraffe. Oh! what a knee . . . now the legs, here is a thin leg with a heel." The procedure for creating body and legs was one of piecemeal addition, sticking thin strips of dough closely together. Abe's second figure evolved in the following manner: "First I'll make her a long neck, like Daddy's. I'll make it very long, looks like cheese . . . Here is her head, now the eyebrows, now the eyes . . . what a small eye, I made it like a crumb, here is her mouth. She has more parts, a neck with bones, and here are legs like Daddy's."

56. Stick figures, continued (boy 4-8).

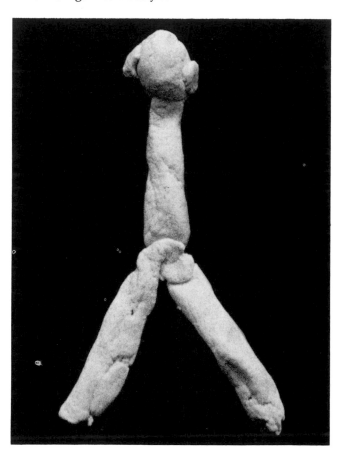

Piecemeal addition of dough pieces is not limited
to the stick-model. Figures 55, 56, 57, and 58, for
example, display bodies created as single units by
rolling dough into long sausage-shapes and flattening
them lightly.

The adoption of a graphic model in playdough
does not imply its continued use. On the contrary,
the child who spends a great deal of time with this
medium tends to discard the less suitable model and
invent other means of representation. For example,

*57. Stick figures,
continued (girl 4-9).*

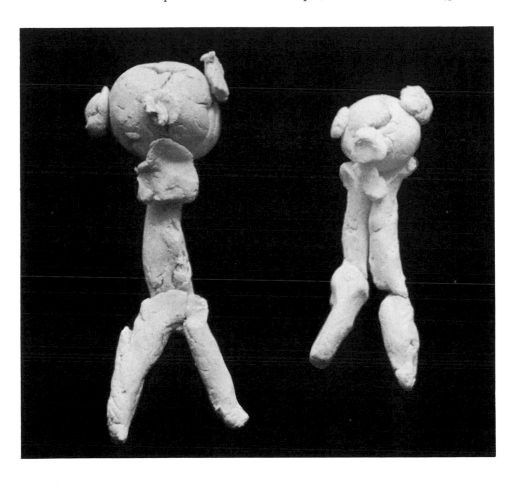

Growth and Differentiation

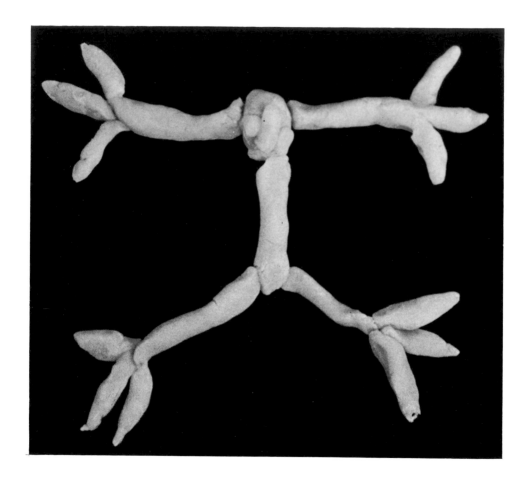

58. *Stick figures,*
continued (girl 5-4).

Young Children's Sculpture and Drawing

the graphic model in playdough is unstable: it cannot be lifted without serious dislocation of parts and it requires patience and fine motor coordination; for these reasons it may be exchanged for a different model. Above all, models should be considered as tentative solutions, temporary formulas for representation.

Working with an unfamiliar or new medium presents a challenge, and most youngsters experiment with the medium and learn as they explore. This leads to spontaneous discoveries of new models and to their improvement, and at times to the adaptation of two-dimensional models to the three-dimensional medium. Observing the child's exploration of the new material we can witness quite dramatic instances of progress in representation.

The first attempt of Hai (5-1) to model a person resulted in the formation of three balls, vertically aligned but detached from each other. These represented head, body, and legs respectively. His second effort led to a similar configuration, but this time the two lower balls were adjoining. On the third try the shape of the tummy changed to a slightly flattened oval. On the fourth, Hai made two erect, standing legs, connected by a horizontal bar; this structure was destroyed. Next, he rounded a piece for the head and attached an oval-shaped part under it, which he described as "it ends the tummy." This was followed by a bulky and protruding piece, the tummy, and a long snake-type formation representing the legs. All of the modeled parts were solidly attached as illustrated in Figure 59.

Another example of learning by exploration can be seen in the case of Meir (4-7). His first trial was limited to pressing and pushing the dough while holding it in his hands. He showed no evidence of planned action and, finally, in an effort to end the task, offered the unformed blob of dough, "look, here is the doll," followed by his admission "can't do it."

Growth and Differentiation

*59. Horizontal figure
composed of several
solid parts (boy 5-1).*

On the second attempt, he fastened both hands
around the dough, squeezing and lengthening it into
an elongated form. He stood the figure up, lengthened
it some more by stretching the dough, and designated
the parts: head, tummy, legs. On his third try Meir
deliberately shaped the dough into a lengthened blob,
pinched the top part to indicate the head and
remarked: "A fat mummy, she ate too much"
(Figure 43).

In many instances, a child starts out with a global
representation of a human—a disk with some

indentations, for example—and within a single session progresses to a tadpole figure or even a figure consisting of three parts. Frequently, the first structure is flimsy, unstable, and unshapely, and the child improves on the second or third attempt. The first task of Boaz (4-10) was to model a baby. He fumbled with the dough, pressed and turned it, and finally pulled a piece off and rounded it: "I can only make a small baby, just the head . . . here is the body." He placed a flattened piece of dough under the head and attached two thin strips of dough to the body to represent the legs. Next he held the figure up and the flimsy structure collapsed. Boaz reassembled the parts on the table, held the figure up, and remarked critically: "One leg is bigger than the other." His second assignment was to make a mummy. "I know it needs a bigger head, here is her body, a big one—feet like for the baby, just bigger." He modeled a round piece for the head, a flattened one for the body, and two legs. All the parts were modeled on the table, securely attached, and the figure maintained its horizontal posture on the table. The third attempt to model a human (daddy) followed the same procedure, but the pace quickened and the boy displayed greater confidence in his handling ability. "Here is a big head, the body . . . I thought I wouldn't know, but I know" (Figure 60).

Other improvements may concern facial features. On the first trial some children place the features on the face, pressing them into the dough surface until they disappear. On the second and third attempt such procedures may be discarded in favor of raising the features or poking them out.

In other instances a child may discard a graphic model for a solid one, since the latter is more stable and can be lifted or moved without as much difficulty. The reverse also occurs; a child may search for means of differentiation and find that the outline model

Growth and Differentiation

articulates more clearly the several parts of the human figure than the bulky and global sculpture. Some children fail to model a man but, following the more familiar drawing task, apply their graphic model to the playdough. This happened in quite a few instances, with the child transposing his graphic tadpole formula to the three-dimensional medium. The following is an example of a three-dimensional tadpole man who acquired, via drawing, a differentiated torso. Amalia (4-7): "You take a big piece and you make a mummy. Here is a mummy . . . you need a hat too, now the legs." The first ball of dough represented the mummy; the second ball of dough was placed on top of it and served as a hat. Finally Amalia added two short legs under the erect standing figure. After sculpting she drew a person

60. Horizontal figure with well differentiated parts (boy 4-10).

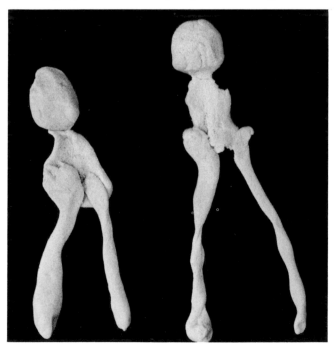

consisting of a head, a graphically distinct body, and legs. Following this she was presented with another portion of playdough and again asked to make a person. This time the figure consisted of a head, a body, and two legs. The position of both figures was upright.

Differentiation of parts in playdough is closely related to the extent of familiarity and practice with the medium. With exposure to the material children gain the necessary experience to handle it and evolve techniques, procedures, and models for the construction of figures. Occasionally we find a regressive trend in representation. This is the case with inexperienced children who revert to earlier modes of representation when the figure does not materialize. The child attempts to maintain his representational intention, but when he fails to produce an explicit form he may waver and fall back upon more primitive devices such as romancing and reading-off in order to make some sense of his work.

The great majority of one unit figures are constructed in a vertical, upright standing posture, while those created by the joining of separately formed parts are placed in a horizontal position. Making an upright standing figure, even the lumpiest of sculptures, involves special difficulties. The figure wobbles and tends to topple over; this is particularly true when its construction involves the joining of parts. Making the sculpture stand up can be very frustrating; drawing is much easier by comparison. One solution to the problem of balancing a standing figure is to place it horizontally on the table. The supine figure is thus determined by two factors: the graphic model and exasperation with constructing a standing one. The overall direction of this type of figure is vertical-horizontal; the figure is constructed in the vertical plane, with arms extended horizontally.

Growth and Differentiation

Compared with the drawn man, the trend in modeling is toward an earlier differentiation of the trunk as a separate structure. However, facial features and other details such as hair, ears, fingers, and toes are less frequently represented in modeling than in drawing. This rule clearly does not apply to the graphic model since it is derived from the two-dimensional medium and retains the distinctly graphic characteristics of representing details.

Most youngsters at this stage of representational development ignore the problem of proportion and relative size of figures. Three-dimensional treatment of the figure is also rare, and children concentrate on the frontal plane of the figure, modeling facial features, bellybuttons, and occasionally hair. The earlier observed trend of creating simple figures persists, and the young artists seem to follow the rule that the bare minimum necessary to achieve perceptual likeness will do. Thus, a new balance obtains between the need to differentiate the figure and the persistent tendency to economize and simplify. Children frankly express their awareness of features which could be represented, but declare that they won't make them and that the figure can do without these parts. Judy (4-11): "I won't add arms; it is too much . . . I am not going to make his hair, we'll pretend that it has hair." Aby (5-2) made an erect standing tadpole man and explained: "Here is his little eye . . . I don't have to make the nose, no space."

The difficulty of modeling tends to reinforce the inclination toward economy and simplicity in representation. Moreover, the child's attitude is characterized by a fair share of playfulness and a freedom to symbolize and transform the parts he has created. This playfulness permits the child to resign himself to the imperfections of his sculpture, to rename, to reinterpret, and to qualify his final product instead of reworking it. Peter (4-0) modeled a figure

Young Children's Sculpture and Drawing

consisting of a head, facial features, and hair. ". . . [hair] sticking up, needs legs, I can pull some out, but they are tiny, if I pull more they will break." Eric (4-11) made a solid head with facial features, an outline trunk, arms, and legs. Upon inspection he reinterpreted the figure as follows: "I cut out the insides of the giant so now he is dead."

When the legs turn out unequal in length, children tend to "explain" this inequality rather than correct it. Common interpretations are: "he broke his leg," "just came from the hospital," "got chopped off, "his leg got shot." When the head is too small to hold all the important facial features, we witness the displacement of parts, for example, the mouth sinks down and comes to rest on the torso as illustrated in Figure 57. Statements such as "his hand turned out awfully big," "what a long finger I made," "I won't make the fingers you can do without them" reflect the young artists' resignation over the imperfect state of affairs.

From the child's remarks we have learned that he is an astute observer of his own work, at times critical and dissatisfied but always ready to reinterpret the work rather than search for an alternative method that would bring his figure closer to the adult's "realistic" conception. The youngster displays freedom from such constraints, license to include a feature or leave it out much as he pleases, so long as the basic structural requirements are met. These requirements change with age, experience, and developmental level. The four-year-old's interpretation of his work transforms the irregularity of the figure without abandoning his original representational intention. It is a playful and imaginative transformation that achieves its aim of making sense of the figure. The child does not accept the erratic nor does he modify it by modeling procedures; he eliminates the contradictions by playful and narrative tactics. Thus he strikes a

Growth and Differentiation

compromise between fact and fancy, and for the time being this represents a satisfying solution. A dynamic balance is maintained between representational intention, modeling efforts, and playful transformation. The older child will not be satisfied with this kind of resolution. His requirements will be more demanding and he will attempt to fit the figure more rigorously to his standard of correct representation. In spite of the younger child's reliance on interpretations rather than corrections, notice his tremendous progress in representation per se. Interpretations no longer serve as substitutes for modeling; they are reduced to the status of corrective devices.

How do representations in the two mediums compare? I have mentioned in passing some similarities and differences between modeling and drawing. Let us now take a closer look. When we compare an individual child's drawing and sculpture of a human we can distinguish between those who adopt a similar and those who develop a different model for the two mediums. Children who adopt a graphic formula and apply it to the three-dimensional medium tend to use similar models for drawing and sculpting. This applies to some of the tadpole figures and to the figure with the "open" trunk. One four-year-old boy made his playdough man in the form of an upright standing snake, while his drawn people consisted of lines drawn across the paper. Father and mother were represented by long lines, extending over the whole page; children were drawn as shorter lines. The puzzlelike human of Figure 52 is very similar to the drawing made by the same child. This youngster, however, made a "garden" consisting of a basket-type formation with three upright standing columns. This difference in approach to the three-dimensional tasks of making a man and a garden was revealed accidentally when the child misunderstood the instruction. At times the sculpted model improves the drawn version of a man. Awy (4-8) modeled the human represented in Figure 55. His drawings consisted of a head and three lines. Two lines represented the legs and the third one stood for the tummy. Since all three lines overlap, the end result is a visually crowded and somewhat incongruent structure. He repeated this version two more times and only on the fourth drawing did he attain the visual clarity and articulation of the sculpted figure.

Differences between the graphic and the plastic model can be quite striking and reflect the influence of the medium on the representational conception. Orith (3-9) made a one-unit sculpture consisting of a blob of dough with pinched out limbs and indented eyes (Figure 44). Her drawing of a person lacked both head and body contour; it consisted of eyes, nose, mouth, arms, and legs (Figure 61a).

Eli (5-3) constructed his man from several parts. First he made the head and attached two arms to it, followed by the body, and finally the legs (Figure 62). His drawing of a person lacks both head and body contour; the tummy is represented as a scribble under the facial features and between the limbs (Figure 61b).

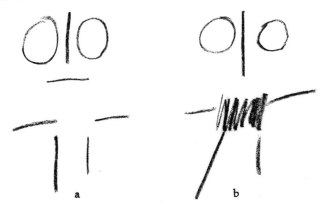

61. *Contourless models (girl 3-9, boy 4-10); artist's sketch.*

a   b

Growth and Differentiation

Judy (4-0) drew a simple tadpole man consisting of head, facial features, and two verticals. Her sculpted man is a well-differentiated figure: "I'll give him a little bow, he is getting dressed up. I'll make his chest, his legs, his feet. Here are his pants. Now I'll make him arms. He doesn't like them; I'll make him little arms and hands." She modeled all the parts

62. Fully differentiated horizontal model with head, trunk, and limbs (girl 5-2).

Young Children's Sculpture and Drawing

mentioned and created an articulate, complex figure.

Yona (5-1) drew a figure consisting of several detached parts: head, legs, feet and body (Figure 24, right). Unlike the drawing, her playdough figure consists of head, body, and legs, all firmly attached (Figure 95).

Some of the stick-models in playdough are matched with a quite different drawn model. Eugenia (4-9) modeled a stick-man of playdough (Figure 55) with arms extending from the body. Her drawing consists of a large circle with facial features, arms, and legs extending from the circle. She located the tummy inside the circle which reveals the compelling logic of the placement of the arms. Drawing the arms from the body-contour is quite consistent with her representational conception.

An intriguing difference between drawing and modeling can be observed in the work of Hagit (5-10), who drew a graphically well-differentiated figure consisting of face, neck, tummy, arms, fingers, and legs. Her sculpture consisted of a flattened slab of dough on which the facial features, tummy, and legs were "inscribed" (Figure 63 right). Her identical twin sister modeled the very different figure on the left. Hagit's drawing and sculpture can both be considered graphic models though, strangely enough, it is the graphic model in playdough which lacks head and body contours.

In both drawing and modeling the figure whose parts have not been joined is found, though it is more prevalent in the former. Esther (4-9) created two sculptures, a classical stick-model and a body composed of two "sticks." The several parts are attached carefully (Figure 57). Her drawing of a man consists of a head and a contour which envelopes head and body area without adjoining them (Figure 64).

The trunk as a separate structure develops earlier in modeling than in drawing. In drawing it may be

Growth and Differentiation

implied by a scribble, a bellybutton, a circle drawn between the two verticals, or by lengthening the outlines of the figure. Apparently, playdough as a three-dimensional medium requires somewhat different means of representation.

Individual differences in representing the human figure are pronounced. Some young three-year-olds (3-0 to 3-5) produce advanced drawings and scuptures, while some four- or even five-year-olds create relatively undifferentiated tadpoles. Nevertheless, the general trend is toward increasing complexity of representation with age. Some children create structurally simple figures consisting of a circle and two lines, but add numerous facial details such as eyes, eyebrows, eyelashes, pupils, nose, mouth, forehead, cheeks, and chin. In general, however, differentiation of parts is closely related to the figure's structural properties. As the child begins to pay more attention to detail, the figure improves in terms of structural organization. Mere representation of parts, for example, is rare if not absent. Given an

63. Diverse models; left figure consists of several solidly formed parts, representing head, trunk, and legs; right ones consist of flattened slabs of dough upon which facial features are "drawn" (twin sisters 5-10).

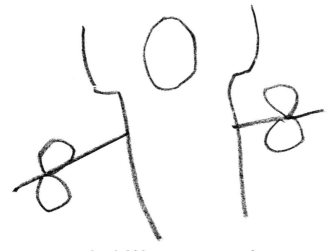

64. Figure with open unattached body contour (girl 4-9); artist's sketch.

opportunity, the child learns to arrange the parts in a visually coherent unit. If an older child persists in the arbitrary placement of parts in spite of continued practice with drawing and modeling, it should be considered a symptom of disturbance. Since practice and freedom to explore the mediums are crucial for representational achievement, lack of such experience will retard the child's performance, at least temporarily. In Chapter 5 ways of assessing the ability of the child who lacks experience, and of distinguishing him from the retarded or mentally disturbed child will be discussed.

Our youngster has emerged from the scribble stage, mastered representational forms, and in this process discovered his representational talents. He is faced with the difficulty of the medium and with the task to invent suitable representational models. He does not aspire to copy the object and seems aware that he is engaged in "representation." In the words of Jay (4-4), "How do you make a person of clay? With a pencil it is easier to make . . . You *can't make a real man*, you can't make the bones." Children take great pride in their inventions as Debby (4-4) tells us: "I found out a new way for toes and fingers . . . I thinked and I thinked, and I just thinked it up."

Growth and Differentiation

The Full-Fledged Figure:
The Complete Man

In the course of the child's graphic development the human figure evolved from the all-inclusive circle through the tadpole man to the open-trunk model. As it approaches graphic completion, the figure undergoes further changes. Graphic completion implies that its major parts are distinctly indicated and that new and more articulate solutions to the representational task are adopted. Unquestionably the simple tadpole looks like a human and is usually recognized as such. This figure, however, retains some ambiguity, as illustrated by the "open" trunk. The vertical lines extending from the circle-head represent the legs as well as the body's contour. With the graphic differentiation of the trunk in the shape of a circle, a square, or a triangle, the ambiguity of the earlier representation is overcome and the closed two-dimensional form stands unmistakably for the torso. With separate delineation of such major parts as trunk, arms, fingers, legs, and feet, the drawn figure approaches "completion" in the conventional sense.

After the open-trunk model, the drawn man acquires a differentiated body. Earlier, in the "scribble" trunk of the younger children (Figure 15), one of the precursors of the separately delineated trunk was encountered. Figures 65 and 66 show two more scribble trunks.

A somewhat more advanced and visually more coherent solution than the scribble trunk can be observed in drawings in which the child "closes" the two outlines to indicate where the belly ends. In this case the child, after drawing the verticals, adds a horizontal connecting line to delineate the space taken up by the tummy; Figures 67 and 68 (left) are examples. The curved horizontal line of Figure 68 was drawn after completion of all three drawings— "and now a line to show the dress."

The figure with the open trunk and the small circle between the verticals is a forerunner of the circular

The Full-Fledged Figure

65. *Figure with scribble trunk (girl 3-6).*

66. *Figure with scribble trunk (girl 3-9).*

67. *Figure where the horizontal line connecting the two verticals delineates trunk section (boy 4-6).*

68. *Family. Two figures (center and right) display the graphically incomplete open trunk; the horizontal curved line (left) represents the "dress" (boy 6-0).*

The Full-Fledged Figure

trunk (Figures 18, 23, and 27 middle). When the trunk is drawn as a separate form rather than a continuation of the body-leg contour the circular shape seems to be preferred, as can be seen in Figure 69.

Thus, the child arrives at the separately delineated trunk by two different procedures: by "closing" the outlines and creating a squarish trunk, and by drawing a circular shape under the head. Once the drawn figure develops a differentiated torso, both the circular and the squarish trunk appear with equal frequency. The triangular trunk is a later achievement, appearing between the ages of five and six. Occasionally the old and the new are combined as when a circular trunk is enclosed by a square!

At this stage of graphic development the circular shape is still the easiest and the most familiar one for the child. He shows his preference in many ways. In addition to the circular head, eyes, cheeks, ears, trunk, and buttons many parts are drawn in a sunburst pattern. Eyes and eyelashes, hands and fingers, feet and toes, head and hair are often represented as circles with lines, ovals, or loops irradiating from them. A simplified version of the sunburst pattern is found in the lines which radiate from a single center and frequently serve for hands and feet. The exact number of fingers is—graphically speaking—irrelevant; the radial pattern portrays the perceptual quality of the outstretched hand adequately. The sunburst pattern is a universally preferred form at early stages of graphic development since it combines balance, symmetry, and pleasing appearance with relative ease of drawing. In time this pattern is also used to represent the sun, though it is not derived from it. (This may even be the case with solar disks or the sun-faces of prehistoric rock art; Anati, 1967.)

Young Children's Sculpture and Drawing

69. Figures with circular trunk (children 4-0 to 5-10).

Form at this stage of development is still nonspecific; the circular shape does not stand for roundness per se but for the quality of "thingness," and represents all objects equally well (Arnheim, 1954). The circle is a generalized representational form useful for almost any object and its parts. Only when forms begin to differentiate, that is, when other forms such as the square, rectangle, and triangle come into being, does the circle acquire specificity and become more exclusive in its representational meaning. The process is gradual; already in the tadpole figures indications of form differences and preferences are found. Although the circle represents head and body, lines are preferred for arms and legs and somewhat later come to stand for body contour. Children may continue to use preferred forms even if they clash with their awareness of form requirements. A five-year-old boy drew hair as loops surrounding the head circumference: "I made my sister, but she doesn't really have curly hair."

Younger children who draw tadpole men seem to ignore the live model in front of them. Apparently they do not feel a need to study the object since they know perfectly well what a person looks like. Their ambition is to create simple, general forms of equivalence; they do not aim at photographic likeness. With the need for greater differentiation of the figure and the increasing demand for visual clarity of the drawing we observe in some youngsters the tendency to inspect their own bodies, checking and touching parts such as neck, shoulders, and trunk, and scrutinizing the adult before them.

Up to 50 percent of the figures which display a graphically distinct torso are armless; the figure consists of head, trunk, and legs, emphasizing the human's vertical dimension. These drawings capture the overall perceptual quality of a man quite well, as Figures 70, 71, and 72 illustrate. Figure 72 was

70. *Armless figure (girl 5-2).*

drawn by Eric (5-0), who remarked after inspecting his work: "It's a girl with hair; she can put her head right under it . . . she has a stomach and a dress, she is dancing." His remarks imply that he has noticed that the head is detached from the hair and is trying to justify it.

When arms are drawn, the majority (90 percent) place them at right angles to the torso, thereby creating a structurally articulate horizontal-vertical configuration. As Arnheim has pointed out, the right-angular direction renders the relationship between arms and body in the visually simplest manner. Analogous to the evolution of forms and their gradual differentiation, the representation of direction is only slowly acquired. The early rectangular relationship of arms and body is nonspecific and does not yet represent a particular direction. Only when other directional relations are discovered, and incorporated into the child's repertoire of forms and their orientation, do the right

72. *Armless figure emphasizing the verticality of the human body (boy 5-0).*

71. *Armless figures, continued (children 3-9 to 5-3).*

The Full-Fledged Figure

angular and the oblique relation become specific and begin to represent gesture, action, and change of direction.

A relic from the stage of tadpole configuration can be seen in Figure 73, composed of head, trunk, and legs, with arms extending from the head contour. Figure 70 is well-differentiated in terms of the basic parts of the body, but relative sizes have not yet been considered, and the head tends to be equal in size to or larger than the body.

Further efforts toward graphic completion of the figure result in the addition of hands, feet, buttons, hair, an occasional hat or ribbon, and, somewhat later, the shading in of tummy and limbs. We still encounter familiar models, reminiscent of an earlier phase, which emphasize circularity or linear and rectangular verticality. The linear and rectangular models of Figure 74 (top and bottom respectively) and the stick-models of Figure 75 are more advanced versions of earlier models. Figure 74 (right) represents verticality in a new guise. At this stage, however, linear models appear only infrequently and the two-dimensional representation of the trunk seems generally preferred by the young artists. Arms and legs, however, continue to be drawn as one-dimensional lines.

Gradually the circular shape gives way to experimentation with square, rectangular, and triangular shapes. Experimentation leads to spontaneous differentiation of shapes and to planful action. David (4-8) drew four figures successively within one short session, utilizing both one- and two-dimensional forms (Figure 76). Orly (4-9) drew three figures, applying to the next figure what she had learned from each attempt (Figure 77). (1) "A head and a body; you should make it brown; now the legs, shoes, eyes—you need a larger head; it looks like a daddy." (Head and body were colored in; the eyes

73. *Graphically differentiated figure with arms extending from the head region; a relic from the tadpole drawings (boy 5-6).*

The Full-Fledged Figure

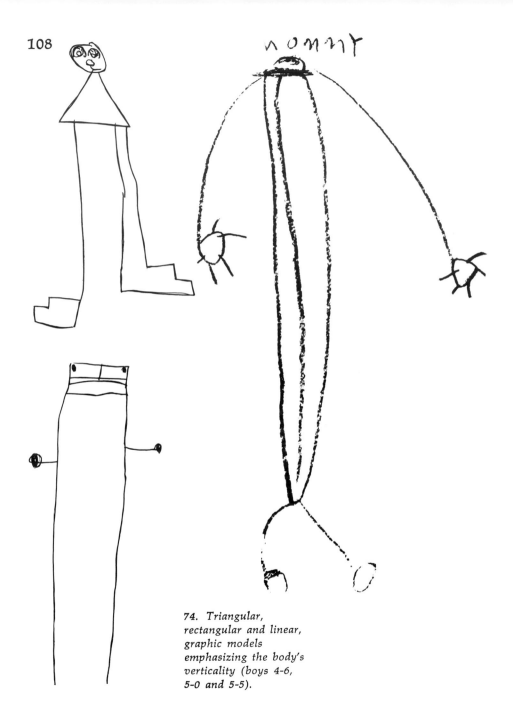

74. Triangular,
rectangular and linear,
graphic models
emphasizing the body's
verticality (boys 4-6,
5-0 and 5-5).

were invisible.) (2) "This time I won't color it in. The body is coming out like this . . . it should be big. I don't have space for the legs; never mind. Now the eyes, and now we can color the rest in." (3) "This time I'll make it beautiful, very pretty. First the legs, head, here the body [a horizontal line is drawn between the verticals]; you should do it this way, now eyes and nose."

75. Stick figures (girls 3-10 to 5-1).

The Full-Fledged Figure

76. Experimentation with graphic forms; four successive attempts to draw the human figure (boy 4-8); artist's sketch.

a   b

The emphasis on exploration and spontaneous differentiation of forms does not negate the importance of learning new ways from siblings, parents, and perhaps even picturebook models. The child learns from others, but within the limits of what makes sense at a given stage of development; he does not learn to draw perspectively from viewing adult paintings. He learns that which is within easy reach and might be discovered all by himself shortly.

As representational forms become more varied, new combinations are tried, preserving some of the older preferences such as circles for head, eyes, ears, and hands and including a rectangular body. Figure 78 shows a clown drawn by a boy (4-7). Figures 79 and 80 are examples of square and rectangular trunks.

The torso becomes further differentiated by a line at the waist, a triangular- or trapezoid-shaped dress, introduction of shirt and pants, and finally the inclusion of the neck. The figure begins to deviate from earlier preferred circular and squarish forms and to show signs of embellishment. It is adorned with

Young Children's Sculpture and Drawing

77. *Successive attempts to draw the human figure leads to distinct improvement in graphic articulation (girl 4-9); artist's sketch.*

78. Clown; imaginative use of the circular shape (boy 4-7).

79. Figures with rectangular trunk (children 4-5 to 5-0).

80. Figures with rectangular trunk, continued (children 4-4 to 6-11).

81. *Figures with triangular trunk (children 5-0 to 7-4).*

82. *Graphic differentiation of the trunk section in the form of a dress (children 4-8 to 5-2).*

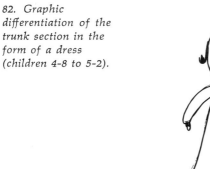

stripes, flowers, buttons, and designs as for the first time the child intends the representation of clothes (Figures 81, 82, and 83).

At this stage children produce drawings skillfully and display a good deal of confidence in their ability to represent the object and meet the demands of the task. The child's conception of the task to draw a man has become more conventional: a man should have a head, a separate body, arms, and legs. Since the main lines are drawn quickly, with motor ease and with pleasure, the young artist can afford to spend time and effort to equip his figure with extras such as hair, shoes, tights, laces, fingers, and pockets. He is willing and even eager to draw whole families, and announces his intention beforehand. His requirements have become more stringent, though he still applies

83. Figures with a differentiated, two-part trunk section depicting shirt, pants, and skirt (children 4-5 to 5-5).

The Full-Fledged Figure

different criteria toward his own work and that of older children or adults. This brief exchange between two girls illustrates criticism of a younger child of an older child's work, though the younger one draws armless creatures and frequently leaves the trunk open. A (4-6): "You made his hair too long and you forgot the stomach." M (6-0): "Silly, you can't see the stomach under the dress." A: "Your people are funny; they touch the sky with their head."

Criticism, interpretation, and reinterpretation still play a supportive role and are invoked to explain accidentals and irregularities. They express the child's recognition that the figure is not always the best possible representation of a certain object. The attempt to reveal the humorous aspect of the drawing persists and reveals the conflict between knowledge of the looks of the object and the tendency to accept the imperfections of the figure. This conflict creates imbalance and tension which impel the child to search for better means and models, and to resolve the conflict by representational rather than by verbal means. Gideon (5-2): "The head did not comes out well; now I'll make the tummy, all of it, legs, shoes, hands . . . I won't make fingers; you can do without them." The urge to draw fingers is apparently too strong, for, in spite of his statement that the figure can do without, he adds them.

When the figure has achieved a satisfactory level of graphic differentiation and can be drawn competently, children are ready to pay attention to differences of size, proportion, form, sex, and direction. Now when the child draws a picture of adults and children on the same page, he is apt to distinguish between the size of the figures and pay some attention to the proportion of the parts. Figures 68, 84, and 85 illustrate these newly acquired skills. The head shrinks relative to the torso, and the torso grows to twice the length of the head. Children

84. *Family. Figures show some degree of size differentiation. Child (center) is drawn smaller than father or mother (girl 5-2).*

85. *Family. Distinct size differences; child is the smallest figure (girl 6-3).*

The Full-Fledged Figure

also indicate their awareness of sex differences by the treatment of hair: a braid or long hair with a curl at its end for girls, short hair for boys. The head contour of the female figure is often represented by long hair and is left partially incomplete as can be seen in Figure 86. (This may in time disappear if the present vogue of unisex hair styles persists.) Distinctive treatment can be observed in the representation of clothes: dresses and jewelry for females, pants and belts for males. The strict horizontal-vertical direction of the figure gives way to the slanting of arms and legs by the drawing of diagonals. This deviation from the right angle increases the complexity of the composition and introduces dynamics into the picture. One-dimensional limbs are slowly transformed to two-dimensional arms and legs. In general the figure is more carefully planned and executed: the size of the head is coordinated more closely with the number of features to be placed inside it, and the latter stay well within their boundaries; the figures are aligned next to each other and no longer seem to float in undefined space; fingers and toes are counted as they are drawn. The human figure gains in complexity as the number of

86. Boy and girl, watercolor (girl 5-0).

Young Children's Sculpture and Drawing

drawn parts increases. Figures 87 and 88 illustrate separate necks drawn on figures.

So far the differentiation of the drawn human has consisted in an increase in the number of depicted parts and construction of the figure by drawing individual parts as self-contained units, one following the other. The figure's completion has been achieved by a procedure of addition, whereby successively created parts are joined into a complex and coherent unit. The simultaneous planning of part and whole culminates in the adoption of a *continuous* outline which fuses the several parts into a closely structured, highly unified whole. The additive procedure which joined head, trunk, and limbs is superseded by the sweeping continuous outline exemplified in Figure 89 (first-graders).

In addition to the structural characteristics described so far, the figure gains in detail with the depiction of irises, pupils, eyelashes, nostrils, hairpins, necklaces, and earrings. Thus, the tendency to economize gives way to the desire to elaborate and to beautify. The first-graders (six- to seven-year-olds) will begin to experiment with side views and attempt to increase the similarity of their portraits to the original model. When drawing they look attentively at their live model and strive to attain likeness by including personal clothing, jewelry, eyeglasses, and so forth. The possibility of drawing profiles is considered. Jonathan (6-10) drew a person and remarked: "Looks very much like me . . . do you want the face looking out of the picture or like they usually are—on the side?" . . . "I don't like it, looks like a fish head."

A word of caution concerning age-norms. Throughout this book I have stressed the value of experience with the medium, the importance of exploration, of interest and pleasure in drawing. The examples in text and illustrations indicate that the

The Full-Fledged Figure

87. *Figures with a graphically distinct neck (children 5-1 to 6-5).*

88. *Figures with a graphically distinct neck, continued (children 5-2 to 5-9).*

89. *Figures drawn with a sweeping continuous outline, fusing the parts into a unified whole* (children 6-2 to 6-9).

121

The Full-Fledged Figure

normal range is wide and that hasty conclusions should not be drawn from a single drawing. Many variables affect the drawing: experience and skill, developmental level, personality, motivation, and the influence of peers and elders. Thus, it is safer to speak about group norms and averages than to assess an individual child's graphic achievement from a single or even a few drawings. In comparing age groups and assigning ascending scores to drawings in terms of structural differentiation we find that median scores increase with age.

Finally, a few spontaneous drawings and paintings have been included to offer the reader a glimpse of the productions children create under conditions of relatively free play in nursery school, kindergarten, or home (Figures 90, 91, 92, and 93). Given freedom to choose colors and tools, the pictures display imagination and boldness which cannot be matched by the simple pencil or crayon drawing of the human figure which is the subject of this inquiry. Magic markers, water colors, and brushes are tricky runaway tools of creation, and the end result is not quite predictable. However, they facilitate the motor aspect of representation and a few dots and splashes easily decorate the picture and express the child's fantasy, mood, and playfulness. By comparison with these independent colorful productions the requested pencil and crayon drawings seem almost "lifeless" or "schematic." Moreover, the free drawing represent many objects, not just the single required one; they hint at the joy of the young artist at work, his sense of aesthetics and form.

As in drawing progress in modeling leads to increased differentiation of the human figure; all the major parts of the body are now quite distinctly modeled. As the playdough figure approaches "completion" we can distinguish the following three models: the upright standing figure, composed of

90. *Girl with decorated dress; hair serves as head contour, watercolor (girl 5-5).*

91. *Children, magic markers (girl 4-0).*

The Full-Fledged Figure

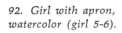

92. Girl with apron, watercolor (girl 5-6).

Young Children's Sculpture and Drawing

93. *Child, crayon*
(girl 4-4).

several solid parts; the outline figure, which is essentially a graphic model; and the horizontal figure constructed of solid rounded or flattened parts, which has the appearance of a compromise.

The primitive one-unit model of Figures 43, 44, 45, 46, and 47 splits apart. At the very least it now boasts a separately formed head placed on top of the body and usually it exhibits legs. The several parts are modeled successively, and each is attached to the one preceding it. The figure is held up or placed upright on the table. The usual construction sequence starts with the head or the legs, though occasionally the trunk is modeled first.

Figure 94 (left) is the work of a girl (5-2). First she modeled the legs, rolling two sausages and attempting to stand them up. They collapsed several times ("legs like a giraffe") until eventually made wide enough to stand upright. Next the young sculptor experimented with the distance between the legs, bringing them closer together to support the tummy. A slightly flattened lump of dough—the tummy—was placed, somewhat sagging, between the legs; a bellybutton was indented; and the figure was

The Full-Fledged Figure

94. Erect models with
head, body, and legs
(girl 5-2, boy 5-9).

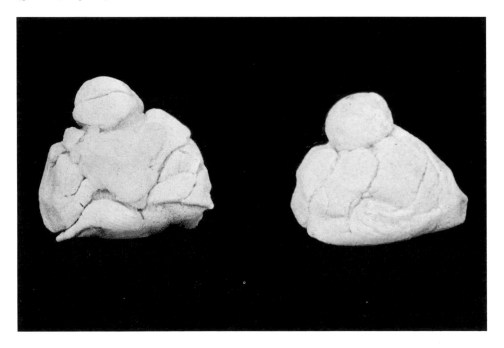

completed by the addition of a rounded head. Facial
features were omitted. The same girl drew Figure 24
(right) in which the several parts of the body are
detached from each other.

Figure 94 (right) was modeled by a boy (5-9). He
held the dough in his hand, pulled a piece off the
lump, rounded it to represent the head, and placed it
on top of the bulky body. Finally he molded a thin
base to serve as legs and attached it underneath the
body. The figure then stood erect.

The armless sculptures of Figure 95 (boy 6-1) and
Figure 96 (boy 6-3) were modeled from the head
down to the legs. During this process they were held
in the hand to emphasize uprightness.

In modeling as well as in drawing we find instances
of self-reference, in which the artist touches his own
body to help clarify the parts to be modeled. Melinda
(4-3): "Gotta make a round head and a flat tummy,
that's the way I have my tummy" (points to her own).
Sammy (4-7): "If I know how to make a doll I can
also make a daddy. You have to make him big . . .
he doesn't have fat legs, just a fat stomach. I can
make the tummy, you make it like this [points to
his own]; it's like an egg, you have to stick 'em on
here, I hold him [up], now we got a daddy." At first
glance the figure seemed complete. Then he checked
his own body, touching and exclaiming: "Ah—it
needs a head, a big head." Promptly he rolled a ball of
dough and placed it on top of the trunk.

While the construction of most figures starts with
either the head or the legs, Figure 97 (boy 5-2) was
developed from its center. The trunk was partially
hollowed out, somewhat resembling a short drinking
glass; a rounded head was placed on top; arms and
legs followed. The faceless figure was held up, then
placed standing upright on the table.

Figure 98 is the third successively modeled figure
by a girl (6-0). Each construction started with the

The Full-Fledged Figure

legs, which during the three attempts grew in size and sturdiness. On each try the young artist next molded the solidly rounded tummy, then arms and head. As the size of the legs increased, the figure gained in stability and its balance improved. All three figures were faceless.

The graphic model in playdough, whose antecedents were discussed earlier in the graphic tadpole figures (Figures 49, 50), persists and is perfected. Instead of

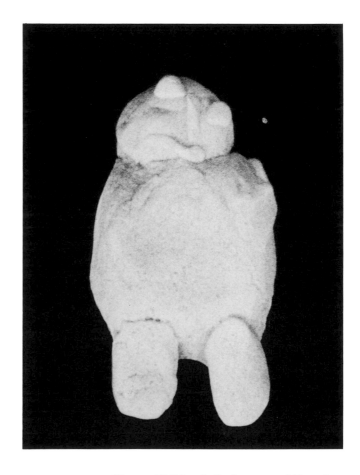

95. Horizontal armless model (boy 6-1).

Young Children's Sculpture and Drawing

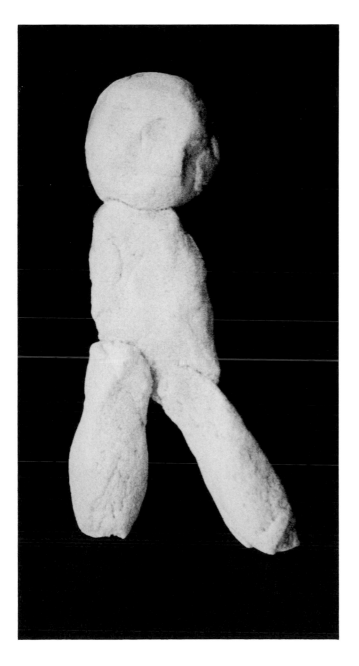

96. *Horizontal armless model, continued (boy 6-3).*

The Full-Fledged Figure

97. Erect faceless model,
(boy 5-2).

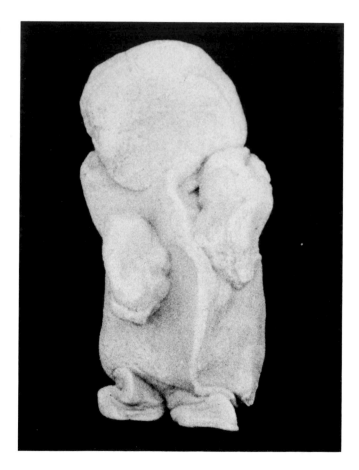

working with solid masses and utilizing the three-dimensional properties of the playdough, the figure is outlined with strips of dough, closely following the characteristics of the drawn line. The head is either a solidly flattened rounded piece of playdough or outlined. In the first the medium properties somewhat modify the strictly graphic model. The trunk is always outlined closely following the graphic model in creating either circular or squarish forms. This model is adopted deliberately as is illustrated by such remarks as, "I'll make it like on paper" or "I'll make it like crayon."

98. Erect faceless model, continued (girl 6-0).

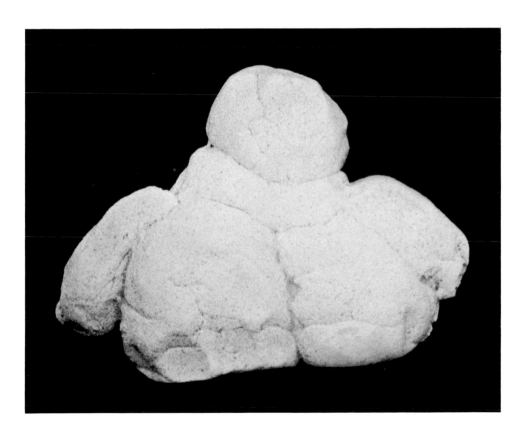

The Full-Fledged Figure

Figure 99 represents a mummy (left) and a daddy (right). The girl (5-6) who modeled them worked the dough while holding the growing figure in her hand. The head of the mother is solid, with large facial features which almost spill over. The two snake-shaped protrusions from the head represent hair; the tummy is circular; the figure, completed by the addition of two legs, is held upright. The figure on the right was similarly constructed. Instead of hair the face boasts a mustache. After completing each figure the artist exlaimed that the mummy (daddy) "looked funny, very odd indeed."

Figure 100 is the work of a girl (5-9), who created the three outline figures in one session. They have solid, faceless heads and outline trunks. The central figure was made first; its arms were modeled after the head and before the trunk. The arms of the other figures were made after the trunk. Note the horizontal-vertical direction of arms and body. All three figures were constructed horizontally on top of the table.

Figure 101 exemplifies the pure transposition of drawn models to the playdough medium. The artist (girl 6-1) applied her graphic models with only slight modification (the solid head of the figure on the left) to the three-dimensional medium. The first figure, a "doll" (left), consists of a solid head with facial features, an outline hat, rectangular outline body, buttons, legs, and feet. The second figure (right), a "mummy," displays a continuous head-body contour typical of drawings of female figures: "Very difficult with long hair . . . a shirt with buttons, legs, and feet." The central figure—a daddy—consists of an outline hat, face and trunk, legs and feet. The three figures are almost identical in form to this child's drawings which she produced subsequent to the modeling task.

99. Graphic models in playdough; circular trunk is outlined with strips of dough (girl 5-6).

The Full-Fledged Figure

The humans of Figure 102 were done successively. That on the right was executed first and displays a tiny circular trunk whose center is taken up by a bellybutton. The figure on the left shows a distinct improvement in its larger trunk; the facial features also include eyebrows.

100. Further graphic models in playdough; rectangular trunk is outlined with strips of dough (girl 5-9).

Young Children's Sculpture and Drawing

101. More graphic
models in playdough;
various forms of
outlining head and body
contours (girl 6-1).

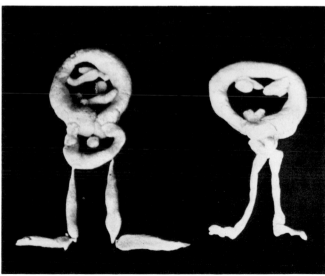

102. Graphic models in
playdough, continued.
Head and body contours
resemble the drawn
figure (girl 6-0).

The Full-Fledged Figure

Graphic models in playdough vary all the way from crude and clumsy versions (Figure 99) to graceful, delicate ones exhibiting a taste for detail and precision. Figure 103 was made by a girl (6-3) who displayed infinite patience in the preparation of the tiny and delicate features, including eyebrows and hair, and attaching them carefully to the small head. She became totally absorbed in her work, willing to correct and reattach those parts which became easily dislodged during the process of construction.

The more robust creatures of Figure 104 were modeled by a girl (5-11) also. The strips extending downward from the head represent the neck, the crossbar stands for the tummy. Note the size differences between the male (left) and the female (right).

Almost all the graphic models in playdough are equipped with distinctive features, and the great majority of them were produced by girls. The figures demonstrate careful planning on the part of their creators, who measure the length of the sides and deliberately choose the quantities to be used, attaining almost perfect symmetry. This work exhibits new constraints and is less playful than that of younger, inexperienced children; a more demanding standard has been adopted by the older artists.

The horizontal figure, composed of solid rounded or flattened parts, seems a compromise formation between the three-dimensional, upright, standing figure and the flat two-dimensional model of graphic origin. Once it develops a differentiated trunk and legs, its appearance and overall workmanship varies from the crude, slightly lumpy, and unshapely construction of the younger children to the skillfully finished and symmetrical composition of the more experienced and older children.

Young Children's Sculpture and Drawing

103. Graphic models in
playdough, continued;
squarish trunks outlined
with thin strips of dough
(girls 6-3 and 6-4).

The Full-Fledged Figure

104. Graphic models in playdough, continued; larger figure is a man, smaller one a woman (girl 5-11).

Figure 105 shows two examples of the work of younger boys, aged 3-9 and 4-4. Figure 106 is the work of a girl (4-1) who had adopted a method of piecemeal addition of tiny bits of playdough to construct her figure; the bits of dough are hammered until they are flattened. In this manner she created a composite structure consisting of face, hair, arms extending from the head, neck, tummy, legs, and shoes.

105. Armless horizontal models with head, trunk, and legs (boys 3-9 and 4-1).

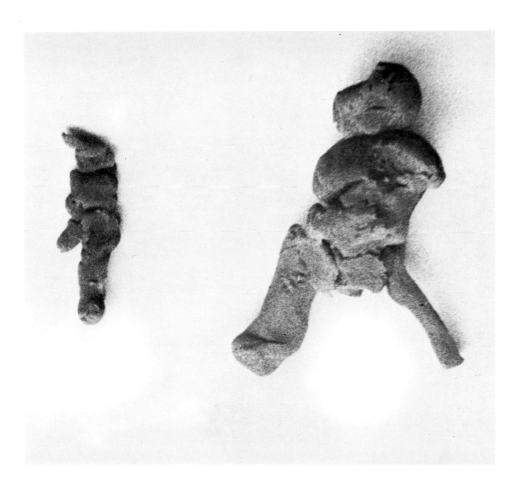

The Full-Fledged Figure

By comparison with the work of younger children (Figures 105, 106), Figure 107 represents the accomplishment of a young craftsman. This sculpture was modeled by an older boy (5-7), who shaped each part separately and to his satisfaction, rolling the required amount of dough for the head, eyes, neck, tummy, and legs. The figure is well-balanced, symmetrical, and of pleasing proportions.

With the acquisition of arms the modeled human reaches a stage of formal completion; the figure has been subdivided into its major parts. The sculptures are constructed with utter simplicity, stripped of detail, and limited to bare essentials; see Figure 108, modeled by a girl (4-8) and Figure 109, modeled by a boy (5-9). Head, body, and limbs are approximately equal in size; the relative proportion of parts has not been considered.

106. Girl, modeled by the addition of flattened bits of playdough (girl 4-1).

Young Children's Sculpture and Drawing

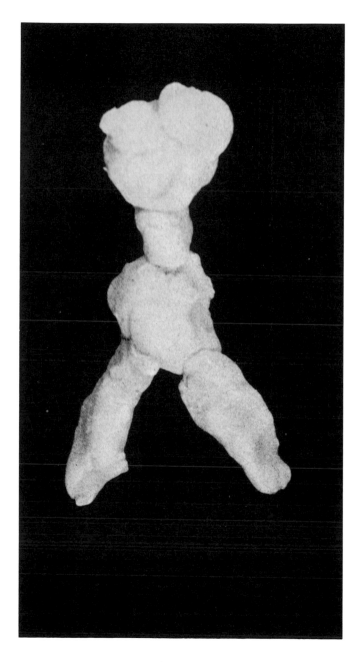

107. Armless horizontal model with head, neck, trunk, and legs (boy 5-7).

The Full-Fledged Figure

142

108. *Horizontal model with clearly differentiated body parts (girl 4-8).*

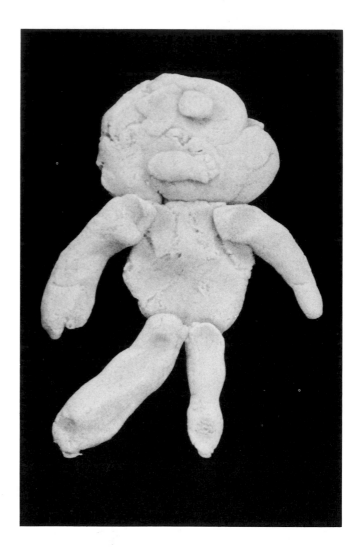

109. *Horizontal model with differentiated body parts, continued (boy 5-9); facing page.*

Young Children's Sculpture and Drawing

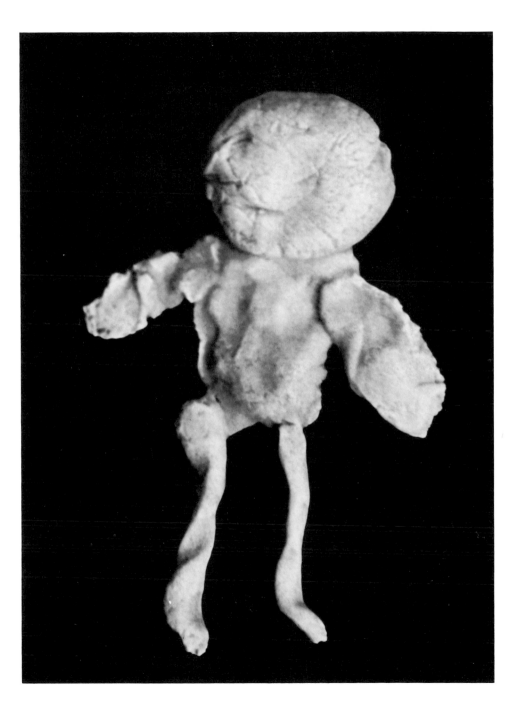

The need for a visually intelligent subdivision of the figure into distinctive parts is the main concern at this stage of modeling; aspects of realistic proportion are generally ignored. When the arms are first endowed with fingers, their size is determined by the zest of creation and need for symmetry rather than by realistic proportions. The modeled parts seem to increase in size as the child proceeds with his work. By the time he models the fingers, which is one of the last acts, he rolls the dough with pleasure and self-assurance, carried away by the activity and enjoying it for its own sake. Most frequently the sun-radial pattern is adopted for the hand and its balanced structure seems to satisfy the child's representational urge. Figure 110 (girl 4-9) demonstrates this interest in the differentiation of forms per se regardless of their relative size. Huge eyes and pupils dominate the face; fingers in the form of a cross adhere strictly to the vertical-horizontal direction of the figure and are arranged in perfect symmetry. In addition to head and arms the figure displays a "throat," legs, and a tummy.

Further examples of the radial hand pattern are illustrated in Figures 111 (boy 5-4), 112 (boy 5-9), and 113 (boy 5-2). The boy who created the last-mentioned expressed his awareness of the excessive size of the hands: "One turned out awfully big." Thus, work habits and the dominance of preferred forms over accurate proportion determine the size of the hands, and emotional significance should not be arbitrarily attributed to them.

A beginning distinction in the relative size of the figures can be seen in Figure 114, modeled by a girl (5-3), who made the child (left) significantly smaller than either father (right) or mother (center). Disproportionately large facial features fill the total facial area.

110. Symmetrical horizontal model with arms extending from the head; figure adheres strictly to a horizontal-vertical direction (girl 4-9).

The Full-Fledged Figure

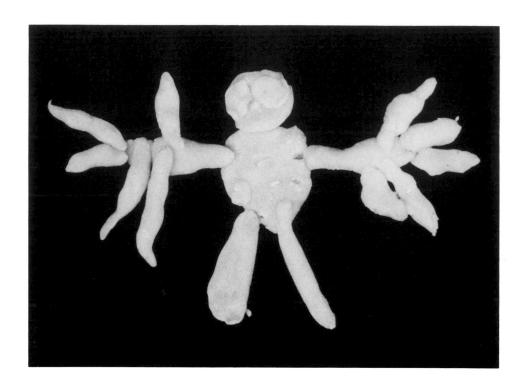

111. Horizontal model with prominent display of radial hand pattern (boy 5-4).

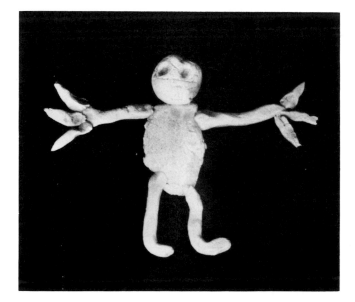

112. Horizontal model with prominent display of radial hand pattern, continued (boy 5-9).

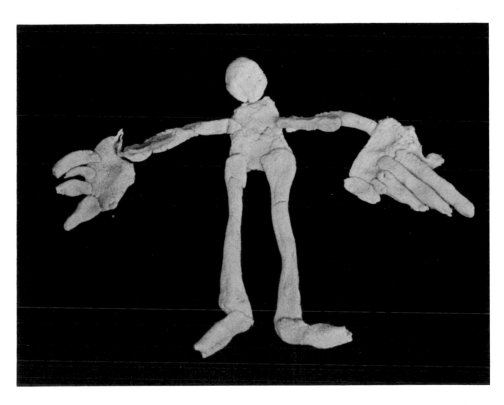

113. Symmetrical horizontal model with large hands and strict adherence to the horizontal-vertical direction (boy 5-2).

The Full-Fledged Figure

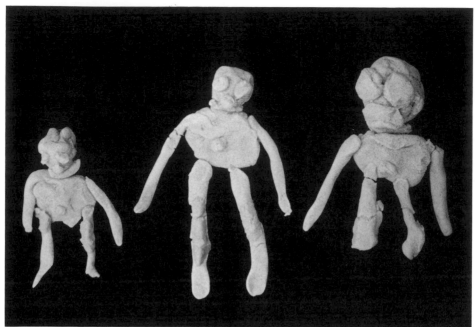

114. Family. Child
(left) is significantly
smaller than adults
(girl 5-3); above.

115. Individual
differences in size of
figures (girls 4-8
and 4-9); below.

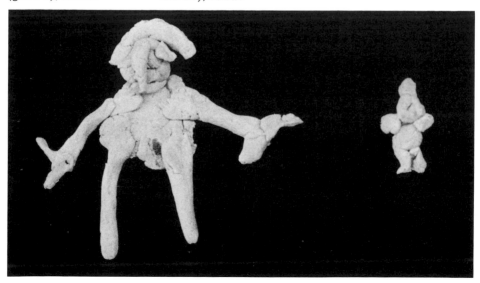

Individual differences in the absolute size of the figures are extreme as can be seen in Figure 115. In terms of structural organization the two sculptures are quite similar, each with a separate trunk, arms, and legs; both are endowed with facial features and hair. They are the work of girls of comparable age, 4-9 and 4-8. The girl who modeled the tiny though perfect figurine (1½ ") drew her humans four times the size of the sculpture. The significance of these individual differences eludes me at this point.

Efforts to differentiate the figure further and to distinguish between the upper and the lower part of the torso can be observed in Figure 116 (boy 5-3). Differentiation of form has been attempted in Figure 117 (boy 5-6), where the male figure displays a rectangular body—a "shirt"—and the female a triangular one—a "dress." The figure in the center represents a doll with a dress.

In each of the three sculpting models the figure passed through a process of orderly differentiation determined by the properties of the medium and the specific model employed. The main emphasis was on the differentiation of forms and the creation of balanced, symmetrical structures. Once this has been achieved, the overall proportions of the figure improve gradually. Up to the age of five, children work on the frontal plane only. Between five and six we find a few instances of turning the figure around, modeling the back lightly or offering verbal recognition of its existence: "The other side is his back and other neck." The dominant directions are horizontal-vertical, similar to those observed in drawing. Along with verbal interpretation of irregularities we now find statements indicating the need for corrective actions: "Have to take some off; finger is too long." Unlike the drawings of this stage, which display many details and embellishments,

The Full-Fledged Figure

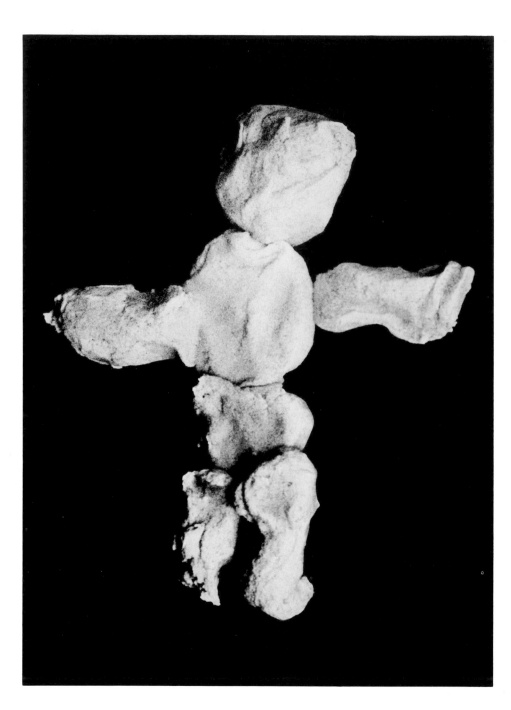

sculptures are composed with utmost simplicity—
by comparison with the drawings one might even
say austerity—although this is not true for the
graphic model in playdough, which closely follows
the drawing style.

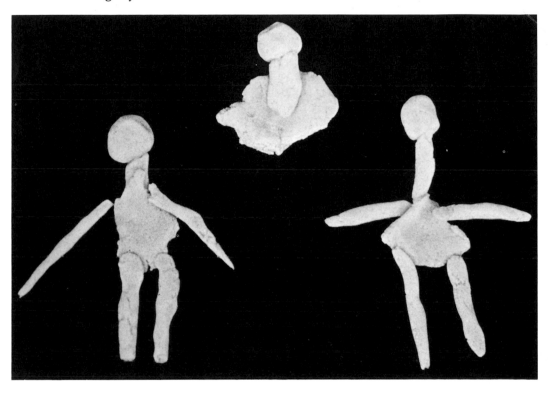

116. Horizontal faceless
figure with distinctly
modeled two-part trunk
and close adherence to
the horizontal-vertical
direction (boy 5-3);
facing page.

117. Faceless figures
marked by a distinct
treatment of the trunk
section: male figure has
a rectangular body, a
"shirt"; female figure a
triangular trunk, a
"dress"; figure in the
center is a doll with a
"dress" (boy 5-6).

The Full-Fledged Figure

The study of drawing on dictation has theoretical as well as practical implications. Unlike free drawing or drawing on request, where the child must decide what parts to represent, on dictation the specific parts and the sequence of their representation are predetermined by the adult instructor. In this experiment I dictated the following parts in the order given: head, eyes, nose, mouth, ears, hair, neck, tummy, legs, feet, arms, and fingers. Drawing on dictation includes neither directions for the spatial arrangement of the parts nor clues for the adoption of specific graphic forms to match the verbal ones. The child is not told where on the paper he is supposed to put the parts or what forms to use. It might be maintained that the mere naming of parts implies a suggestion concerning their placement. If the order is head, eyes, nose, mouth, one might suspect that the temporal sequence could indicate a certain spatial order, from the top down, though the mere naming of them does not specify whether they should be drawn inside or outside the circle-head. Moreover, when parts such as ears, hair, and neck are dictated, the order obviously deviates from the "natural" top-to-bottom sequence. Thus, dictation enables us to assess a child's ability to relate spatially the several parts of the human figure and, simultaneously, to follow the evolution of these forms and their representational significance.

Drawing on dictation is designed to elicit the child's repertoire of forms, and is also useful in assessing his developmental level. In the case of the scribbler who produces only nonrepresentational formations in the drawing task, dictation probes the child's readiness to invent graphic forms to match the verbal ones. In general, dictation tends to provoke the emergence of forms and shed light on the early representational usage of lines.

Human Figure Drawing on Dictation

The majority of those three-year-olds who produce nonfigural designs during the drawing task create on dictation a recognizable and spatially coherent representation of the human figure. Frequently, however, the lines are unsteady and reveal the child's uncertainty and lack of drawing experience. The scribbling child who on dictation produces a graphically differentiated figure has reached a state of representational readiness; after a few trials he usaully can master basic forms such as the circle, and is ready to make the transition to the spontaneous representation of simple forms and figures. Conversely, if on dictation the child succeeds only in drawing line formations, for example, long parallel running lines or short and closely patterned ones, we are dealing with a nonrepresentational child. In the latter case the youngster does not yet grasp the representational character of lines nor has he discovered the basic circular form which is the cornerstone of such representational activity.

Children who are on the verge of representation yet continue to produce scribble lines rather than loops, spirals, circles, and ovals are handicapped in the dictation task. On dictation they may draw two extended diagonal lines that approach closure at the ends, and rely on verbal designation of the top as the head, the center as the tummy, and the bottom as the legs. In this case the child identifies parts according to their location. A slightly more advanced example is the three-year-old boy who drew straight lines for people: a small line for the "child" and long ones for a "fat daddy" and a "fat mummy." On dictation he drew a long line with a tiny circular whirl at the top, arms extending sideways: whirl represented head and glasses, the long vertical line tummy and legs (Figure 118a).

Figure 118b illustrates the work of a boy (4-0) who lacked two-dimensional means of representation

a   b

c

and drew his figure in the form of lines radiating from a center; on dictation he made the transition to representation proper with the purely linear means at his disposal.

Figure 118c shows a man drawn on dictation by a girl (3-6). Her drawings of people consist of a large oval with two circular eyes in the upper part. On dictation she drew eyes, nose, and mouth all properly placed; the neck was represented by a curved line under the oblong while the tummy was drawn *inside* the circular contour. This figure apparently represents a compromise between her own drawing model—the all-inclusive circle—and an attempt induced by the dictation to differentiate the parts outside the circle.

Figure 119a shows what Ray (3-10), a very inexperienced and reluctant young artist, drew. His drawing, which required a great deal of effort,

118. Drawings on dictation (children 3-0 to 4-0); artist's sketch.

Human Figure Drawing on Dictation

consisted of a head, eyes, and curved, detached legs. On dictation he drew the head and facial features but when instructed to draw ears he became tense: "Don't know how to make ears . . . oh! round circles." As further parts were dictated he became ever more frustrated and produced circular scribbles. The task was beyond his experience and exceeded his patience. He was promised a prize if he made a real effort to draw the parts dictated. The result was the surprisingly well-organized man, Figure 119b.

A successful attempt to differentiate the figure over three dictation trials is exemplified in the work of a four-year-old boy. His first drawing on dictation consisted of the all-inclusive circle with the parts drawn inside it. On the second try the dictated parts were more distinctly represented: the head contour bounds the facial features; ears and hair are properly placed; neck, tummy, and legs are arranged in a top-to-bottom order; the neck,

119. Comparison of a free drawing with drawing on dictation (boy 3-10); artist's sketch.

a

b

Young Children's Sculpture and Drawing

however, is detached from head and trunk. Further improvement in the delineation and organization of parts can be observed in the third attempt. The neck is contiguous with the head although still detached from the trunk. All three drawings were made within five minutes (Figure 120).

Scribblers who have mastered closed two-dimensional forms such as circles and ovals are most likely to represent on dictation a fully differentiated figure. Although parts such as head and tummy may be detached on the first trial, they frequently are attached on the second or third. This is the rule for those children who have reached the tadpole stage in drawing; on dictation they usually create fully differentiated and spatially well-organized figures. Figure 121a depicts a crude tadpole drawing by a girl (4-0), who on dictation succeeded in drawing a quite well-differentiated figure (Figure 121b). In a small number of tadpole-drawing children we find a tendency to

120. Graphic differentiation of the human figure on successive dictation trials (boy 4-6).

Human Figure Drawing on Dictation

draw on dictation arms extending from the head rather than from the body—a feature persistently carried over from the drawing model to the dictation task.

Dictation provides a learning experience for the representational child and the one approaching this stage. Children who produce contourless figures on the drawing task (Figure 121c) employ contours on the dictation task (Figure 121d) and are likely to include this new feature when drawing freely (Figure 121e). The drawings of Figure 121c, d, e present the work of a boy (5-3).

Figure 2k is another example of a child's drawing of a contourless human. On dictation the same young artist (3-11) referred to his own body, constantly checking himself: "Where does it go? . . . Is it also a circle? . . . Where is the tummy? Near the head." Unlike the contourless humans of his free drawing, on dictation his figures displayed contours and were graphically well delineated. Above all it is clear that, once the principle of representational outlines is grasped, progress is rapid.

121. Comparison of free drawings with drawings on dictation (girl 4-0, boy 5-3); artist's sketch.

a

b

Young Children's Sculpture and Drawing

With the help of the dictation task one can resolve doubts concerning a child's ability to create orderly spatial relations in his representation. The drawings of one youngster (boy 3-8) consisted of three circularly shaped detached forms which he named head, tummy, and back. The relative position of the parts seemed to indicate representational confusion. Figure 122 depicts his three trials on dictation, revealing his capacity for spontaneous correction and improvement.

Dictation also encourages the child to draw new parts, for example, tummy and neck. The youngster who has never tried to draw a neck is now forced to invent new means of representation. Children tend to solve this problem by drawing a curved line, either contiguous with the head and the trunk, or leaving space between head and neck, and neck and tummy. Some draw the neck as a scribble or in the form of a circle. The neck does not appear in the spontaneous drawings of younger children (up to

c   d   e

Human Figure Drawing on Dictation

age 5-0); it is a new aspect introduced by dictation. Various attempts to represent the neck are illustrated in Figure 123.

The evidence of drawing on dictation supports the analysis of the representational meaning of graphic forms made in the preceding chapters. The function of lines, circles, and scribbles emerges with greater clarity when on dictation the tummy is drawn as a scribble, a circle, or two vertical lines. Marked improvement can be observed in every case where the child is offered a second trial; "open" spaces between the parts tend to be eliminated, detached forms are joined, and the one-dimensional lines used for neck and tummy turn into circular forms. With only two to three tries the figure improves in its overall proportions. It is striking how much learning goes on in a short time.

122. Drawings on dictation; successive trials lead to graphic differentiation of the human figure (boy 3-8); artist's sketch.

tummy

tummy

123. *Graphic solutions on dictation; artist's sketch.*

Drawing on dictation confirms the insights derived from careful observation of young children's drawing behavior (Chapters 1, 2, 3, and 4). It supports my interpretation concerning the evolution of lines for representational purposes; it offers examples of such early form preferences as the circle for the head, the straight lines for the limbs, and the curved line for the neck; above all, it reveals that, in spite of certain form preferences, lines and circles can serve for any or all parts in the early representation of the human figure. At the beginning these forms are nonspecific and have general application.

Drawing on dictation is especially useful in assessing a child's representational readiness. It offers more precise estimates than the free drawing. Repeated dictations reveal the child's capacity to explore the medium and to experiment with forms; they provide a better measure of representational potential than his free drawing. When children persist in drawing immature scribble forms beyond the usual age range of three to four years, drawings on dictation often discriminate between the mentally retarded and the inexperienced youngster. Scribble forms and the arbitrary scattering of disconnected parts in a representation which does not improve over a series of trials may indicate a disturbance of intellectual and/or personality development.

In the past, investigators (Kerschensteiner, 1905; Burt, 1921; Goodenough, 1934) have maintained that the drawings of mentally retarded children lack coherence. It was assumed that these drawings display structural primitiveness, disorganization, and confusion of parts and are characterized by a high incidence of bizarre detail. A recent investigation (Barr-Grossman, 1973), however, reveals that the representational development of the mentally retarded (organically unimpaired) child follows the same orderly progression from the first simple and

global forms to the evolution of increasingly
differentiated figures. Although the retarded child
acquires these representational forms at a slower
rate, the developmental sequence follows the same
pattern as that observed in the normal child.

The reader may recall from Chapter 3 the amusing
"tadpole" creatures which inspired the theories of
several distinguished authors on children's art and
were characterized as typical offspring of the child's
syncretistic and confused mind. In the light of
new findings resulting from the drawing on
dictation task and revealing remarkable spatial
organization of parts—even in the case of
three-year-olds—the interpretation of the "tadpole"
drawings in terms of syncretism and conceptual
confusion has to be discarded. Most of the
youngsters who on the drawing task create only
scribbles or global figures, produce on dictation a
complete figure composed of all dictated parts,
usually preserving fairly correct spatial relations
between them. Thus the study of children's figures
drawn on dictation provides further evidence for an
interpretation of the tadpoles in terms of graphic
models rather than defective copies of the object.
Since both the free drawing and the drawing on
dictation involve the same perceptual-motor skills,
the difference in degree of completion of the human
figure and its coherence cannot be ascribed to
motor skill per se. Why, then, are the drawings on
dictation so vastly superior? The answer seems to
lie in the different structures of the two situations
or tasks. Dictation provides the child with "verbal
parts" which seem to facilitate the representational
process. He still has to invent graphic forms to
match the verbal ones, to recognize these forms
(lines) as adequate representations, and to relate
them to each other and to the whole spatially.
However, the important step of defining parts has
been facilitated, simplifying this complex process.

Human Figure Drawing on Dictation

6 The Human Figure in Puzzles, Completion Drawings, and Snowman Models

The findings described in the previous chapter highlight unsuspected representational abilities in the three-year-old child who produces nonfigural designs or draws only simple global humans. On dictation the drawn lines frequently are unsteady and reveal the child's uncertainty, inexperience, and lack of the fine motor skill which is a prerequisite for this task. The truly remarkable result is the fact that an apparently nonrepresentational child or mere beginner has created a spatially well-coordinated figure. The mere provision of verbal parts enables him to represent in a fairly coherent manner his graphic version of a man.

If the invention or creation of parts plays such a crucial role in representation, and if the provision of verbal parts facilitates this task markedly, can the same effect be produced by presenting the child with simple geometric parts which bear no resemblance to the human body? The answer is affirmative. When confronted with a collection of seven geometric pieces—one disk, two squares, and four sticks—and instructed to make a person, the great majority of three- and four-year-olds construct a complete figure consisting of head, body, arms, and legs (Golomb, 1969, 1973). Tadpole figures, though they dominate the drawings, are extremely rare in this puzzle task. Altogether the puzzle figures surpass the drawn figure in degree of differentiation and organization of the parts and the whole. A child (3-7) who drew a crude tadpole figure consisting of head and appendages made an ingenious puzzle figure: "He is folding his legs under his tummy."

The puzzle task is a fairly unfamiliar one for the youngsters and requires time to be explored. In this experiment the children were allowed three trials, and on the second and third they were encouraged to try something different. Typical comments are: "Can these [sticks] be legs?" "Can these [squares] be anything?" "I am still using the circle as the head." Figure 124 shows various solutions.

When in one experiment the number of puzzle parts is increased to sixteen, and several other geometric shapes are included, the results are essentially the same as with the seven-piece form puzzle. Children respond to the sixteen-piece form puzzle with increased enthusiasm and with bold imagination. The disk is generally chosen for the head, but it is not unusual to find children designating a square as the head and stating so explicitly: "For now this is going to be the head." The typical youngster seems to have no difficulty in "transforming" geometric shapes with little or no resemblance to the human body to serve as body parts for his puzzle man.

The child's attitude toward the puzzle task is altogether different from that displayed toward drawing. Youngsters who are unperturbed by their imperfect drawings and affirm that their simple figure "has enough and doesn't need any more" spend time and concentrated effort to fit the parts together. The puzzle seems to elicit a businesslike attitude: the figure must be equipped with a head, a separate body, and limbs.

Unlike the drawing task, the puzzle task provides the child with ready-made forms, with what one might consider as the very first step of the representational process. The next step the child takes on his own: he creates the "equivalence" between the wooden forms and the object he intends to represent. He "identifies" the parts and places them in relationship to each other. A square piece no longer is a "square," but functions as a particular body part within the context of constructing the figure. Any form, whether square, circle, or rectangle, can serve as "part" for a man. Certain ones are preferred, for example, the disk for "head" and sticks for "limbs." The puzzle does not demand the intense concentration on facial detail so crucial for the drawing task. It also involves less motor effort, since the pieces need only be pushed into what the child considers their proper places. In this task children strive to attain balance and symmetry. They measure the length of the sticks which serve as limbs, rule out unequal lengths, and in general display a more exacting attitude toward this task than toward the drawing situation.

124. Various models of the human figure with puzzle parts; artist's sketch.

Most common forms

Frequent forms

Occasional solutions

Puzzles, Completion Drawings, Snowman Models

If we compare the child's performance on the puzzle and dictation tasks, we find no significant differences between the figures created. To name a part as in dictation or to provide a part as in the puzzle seems to facilitate the representational process for the younger children, who are in a transitional phase between scribbling and drawing or have merely begun representational experimentation and create very simple global figures or tadpole men. Another similarity between the two tasks concerns generality of forms, the almost indiscriminate employment of shapes and the lack of specificity in their use. In the form puzzle any piece can represent a body part—much like the circle in the dictation, which also stands for almost any body part. Whether the examiner *names* a part without supplying a form, or supplies a form without naming it seems to produce similar results.

The effect of the provision of parts on representation can also be explored by providing the youngsters with a limited number of parts, for example, an incomplete representation of the human figure. In this study the incomplete figures consist of (a) a circle with facial features, (b) a face with legs, and (c) a face with arms, legs, and feet (Figure 125).

When we compare children's completions of the three figures, we discover dramatic differences indicating that the figures elicit selective responses. Figure (a), the most incomplete representation of a human, is completed in a more detailed fashion than (b) and (c), partly because it receives a graphically distinct trunk which is assumed to be present in (b) and (c). Some children draw a circular trunk for (a), "close" the trunk for (b), and leave the "open" trunk of (c) unaltered because it is implied between

the two verticals (Figures 126, 127). It is remarkable
that about half of the first-graders consider (c) a
fairly complete human who does not lack a trunk!
These results indicate that youngsters respond
selectively to what one might define as the figure's
"demand characteristics" (Golomb, 1973).

Of particular interest is the fact that the three-
to four-year-olds consistently complete (a) at a
level higher than that of their own drawing of a man.
The great majority who draw only global men or
simple tadpoles complete (a) by adding a trunk and
legs—and some add arms, fingers, and feet. Even
when the head contour is deleted or the facial
features are reduced to the eyes, the demand
characteristic of these figures is essentially the same
and yields similar completions. Altogether, the
completion drawings reveal a higher degree of
differentiation than the human figure drawings.
Evidently the incomplete figure demands a more
complete representation than the purely verbal task
to draw a person literally "from scratch." Older
children, however, who have evolved useful graphic
techniques and patterns and draw a complete though
simple figure, complete (a) according to their own
drawing schema. The term "drawing schema" or
"graphic formula" does not imply a rigid or
immutable pattern; it refers to the temporary
adoption of a graphic configuration which the child
evolves at certain stages of his development.

In summary, the incomplete drawings, which
present the child with a number of ready-made forms
or patterns, have a definite effect on the degree of
completeness of his representation. The child does
not start from scratch; consequently, his performance
on the completion task is usually superior to his
drawings. Apparently the structured materials and
the providing of a limited number of parts
facilitates the representational process.

Puzzles, Completion Drawings, Snowman Models

125. Schematic drawings of the human figure with varying degrees of graphic completion. Figures were used in the drawing completion task.

126. Selective completions of incomplete figures (girl 4-4); artist's sketch.

Young Children's Sculpture and Drawing

127. Selective completions of incomplete figures, continued (boy 4-7); artist's sketch.

Puzzles, Completion Drawings, Snowman Models

Finally we shall consider a somewhat different model of a human: the playdough snowman. The great majority of snowmen consist of several "balls" of dough piled on top of each other, standing in an upright position. The scultpures of the three- to four-year-olds are usually upright and bulky and comprise two to three spheres of dough, rounded forms identified as head and body, or head, tummy, and bottom. Approximately half of these youngsters construct a simple but complete snowman. The tummy is modeled in all cases. The task, though not considered easy, seems relatively clear to the child. Even the younger children seem able to devise a strategy to execute the task. Jef (3-10) rolls five separate balls and stacks them: "Gotta keep making balls, put them on." Jen (3-10): "Gonna have three balls with no arms; snowman have no arm." Deb (3-10): "Make the head, make the bottom first. Now the middle-sized on top of it, and now the head." Jo (3-7) models three balls of dough: "Just to make it on top of each other." Pet (4-0): "Is a baby snowman, snowmen have no legs." Phil (4-3): "Is a melting snowman lying on table." Bo (4-3): "Is a melting snowman is so small."

Among the four- to five-year-olds there is a decrease in the upright, standing snowman; only one-half of these figures are constructed in an upright position. Those constructed in the horizontal plane consist mainly of bulky, rounded forms; a few are flattened to disks. Some snowmen acquire arms, a few feet. The flattened and horizontally placed figures begin to resemble the sculptures of a man and reflect the procedure illustrated by Tim (4-11), who models a head, body, and arms: "The same way you make a man. I don't have enough for the legs, but a snowman doesn't have feet; don't make feet." An interesting finding concerns the snowman's posture. If the snowman figure is modeled prior to the man, there is a sharp rise in its upright posture.

Young Children's Sculpture and Drawing

Apparently, the model of the man influences the snowman production, an influence which can be countered by reversing the order of the two sculpting tasks.

The incidence of upright snowmen increases with the kindergartners (aged five to six), who produce predominantly standing figures. The simple snowman figure begins to show signs of embellishment such as hats, buttons, and sticks. The trend to adopt a "man" model persists in a minority of cases. First-graders (six to seven years) introduce new adornments such as pipes, carrot noses, scarfs, and shovels. Some of their sculptures are very elaborate and for technical reasons constructed horizontally on the tabletop. Figure 128 illustrates several types of snowman figures.

In general the snowman figure seems to evoke a different model from those discussed so far, one not much influenced by the "drawn" or "sculpted" man. The differences concern not only the posture of the figure but also the forms employed for this task. The great majority of snowman figures,

128. Erect snowman models (children 3-5 to 6-3).

including those of even the younger children, boast a separate trunk section; though approximately half of the youngsters do not yet model a separate trunk for their figure of a man, and only a minority of three- to four-year-olds include one in their drawn version of a man. Figure 129 illustrates two sculptures by a four-year-old child. The snowman is an upright, standing figure consisting of three balls of dough. The man has a flattened head (with raised facial features which include eyes, eyebrows, nose, and mouth), an "open" trunk, legs, feet, and arms. This artist uses two distinct models and procedures for the creation of the figures. Altogether it seems that the modeling of a snowman is somewhat easier than the modeling of a man, since *qua formula* the task is better defined, the child knows what kind of a man and what kind of forms he is supposed to make. Essentially the snowman is already a "representation," and its structural demands are relatively easy.

A comparison of young children's representation of the human figure in drawing and modeling, dictation, completion, and puzzles brings out a

129. Different models in playdough. The snowman is a faceless, upright figure, constructed of three balls. The man has a flattened head with raised facial features, open trunk, arms, and legs. Both figures were modeled by the same child (boy 4-4).

remarkable variety of representational models and dispels the misconception that children develop rigid "schemata" related primarily to their developmental level. According to this mistaken view, the child develops a schema which he applies uniformly whenever the task requires him to make a man, regardless of the medium, the demand characteristics of the specific task, the provision of forms, and the extent of practice. This study, however, resulted in the discovery of the evolution of *diverse* human figures in drawing and in modeling, differences directly related to the effects of a two- and a three-dimensional medium. In addition to differences attributable to the properties of the medium, I encountered distinct models of the human in the same medium, such as the snowman and the man of playdough. Moreover, when the child is provided with ready-made forms, as in the dictation and form puzzle tasks, the human figure attains its most complete and articulate representation. The completion task highlights another factor: the selective demand characteristic of incomplete figures.

The most compelling conclusion that can be drawn from these findings concerns the absence of a uniform representational schema, model, or procedure. The overall differentiation of the figure and its degree of completion depend on a variety of factors, on the medium and practice, parts provided or to be created, the demand characteristic of the task, and the child's developmental level. Further analysis of the results reveals an age factor: differences in the representation of the human figure are greatest in the younger children and tend to diminish gradually so that some of the originally distinctive tasks become similar with respect to the construction and completion of the human figure. This occurs, for example, when graphic models are created, perfected, and then applied to other tasks, overruling the earlier distinct character of the different tasks.

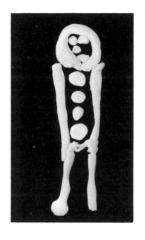

In the preceding chapters we have followed the child in his attempt to create a recognizable representation of the human figure. The behavior of the youngest subjects indicate that they are unaware of the representational possibilities of the medium and do not look for meaningful forms in their accidentally created products. They treat paper and playdough as material quite suitable for their action games. The young child's sheer pleasure in action for action's sake and fleeting interest in the visual results of his motor efforts define this stage as essentially nonpictorial, and as a mere precursor of representational development. With the discovery of the expressive character of lines and dough-shapes, however, comes the recognition of the first meaningful forms and their creation.

The first representational forms, which emerge gradually from the child's scribble exercises and manipulations of the playdough, are crude shapes requiring his verbal interpretation to make them intelligible. Often they serve as points of departure for telling stories, giving rein to playful imagination. At times children conjure up fantastic stories about favorite figures—dinosaurs, monsters, robots, or spaceships—not confining themselves to the drawn or modeled figure but transforming the task into symbolic play. The three-year-old who makes up stories while interpreting his figure modifies the representation in the direction of play and fairytales; fantasy is substituted for planful action. Indeed, the progression from the early prerepresentational substitutions for representation to the reinterpretations which verbally complete the figure or correct its perceived deficiencies parallels the child's growing representational skills and reflects his developing capacity to bring intention, conception, and workmanship into a closer alliance. Eventually the child's representational means

Overview

are developed enough for him to discard verbal interpretations or relegate them to a subordinate role.

The first representational forms serve many purposes, only very gradually acquiring specificity. Indeed, representational development proceeds from an absolute freedom from conventions and lack of specificity in the choice of forms, their orientation and placement on the page, to a representation increasingly determined by a spatial framework and by objective relationships, distinctive forms, and orientation. It is remarkable, however, that even at the early stages of representational development, a certain internal order and visual coherence in the organization of the figure is maintained, for example, in the global man or the tadpole figure. Although these figures, from the perspective of the adult observer, seem to float in space, defying gravity, the relation among the different parts is rather well preserved; for example, the facial features are placed close together, usually inside the circle, or follow a top-to-bottom order in the verbal designation of parts in modeling.

The terms "syncretism" and "juxtaposition" of parts have often been applied to young children's drawings, implying a certain degree of conceptual immaturity and confusion which leads to omissions and such misrepresentations as displacement, condensation, and substitution of parts. The results of this study, however, indicate clearly that a child's representation of a person varies as a function of the specific task and the medium employed. Indeed, the structural complexity of the figure varies significantly in such tasks as drawing, modeling, dictation, completion, and puzzles. The different models evolved by the child are usually simple but visually coherent solutions to difficult representational problems.

Young Children's Sculpture and Drawing

In the past preoccupation with the notion of "schemata" has tended to obscure the explorative nature of the child's activities and the wealth of representational symbols he invents and varies. Some children progress in a single session from simple to more differentiated representations of the human figure (see Figures 31, 32, 33), a finding congruent with the idea of experimentation and invention of models rather than the assumption of a sudden increase in the accuracy of the child's concept of a man.

The question arises as to why the child can solve the spatial relations of the puzzle task and create a fairly complete and detailed figure with geometric parts, yet in the drawing task produce a tadpole man. But consider the difficulties a child faces in drawing and modeling. A major difficulty in these tasks seems to be the very *first* representational step, which requires the "creation of forms." When forms are provided, for example, verbally in the dictation task or as geometric shapes in the puzzles, the child displays a hitherto unsuspected ability to organize these forms or parts coherently and to create a more complexly differentiated figure than he achieves in his drawing of a person. The discrepancy between the child's verbal articulation and his representational intention, on the one hand, and, on the other, the striking superiority of his figures when he is provided with "forms" has been amply documented in the preceding chapters and requires a different explanation than that provided by traditional accounts. The appeal to "syncretism" as an explanatory concept stresses the child's limited capacity to analyze the figure into its constituent components and accounts for the early figures in terms of the child's "synthetic incapacity," that is, his inability to relate parts and whole in a representation. However, the proposition of "synthetic incapacity" cannot be applied selectively, affirmed in the case of drawing and denied in the case of dictation and puzzle figures.

The terms syncretism and juxtaposition of parts seem to describe the productions of youngsters who have not yet made the transition from a prerepresentational attitude to representation proper. Prior to the discovery of the representational possibilities of lines on paper, the child is perplexed when faced with the request to "make" something. If he complies and produces his usual scribble formations, the result is an obscure picture requiring an explanation; his narrative inventions are then easily mistaken for syncretistic reasoning.

The relation between graphic representation and cognition has been discussed primarily by students of cognitive development interested in the psychology of children's art. Some have recognized the difficulties of representing three-dimensional solid objects on a two-dimensional plane; however, with few exceptions (Arnheim, 1954; Meili-Dworetzki, 1957), the significance of the medium has not been adequately acknowledged.

The traditional analysis of children's drawings stressed the child's mental immaturity, his conceptual deficiency (Luquet, 1913, 1927; Goodenough, 1926, 1931; Harris, 1963; Piaget, 1951, 1956), the blurred quality of his memory image (Eng, 1931), and, more recently, the static character of his mental image (Piaget, 1971). It has generally been assumed that the child's portrayal of an object revealed his knowledge of that object; consequently, the peculiarities of his figure were considered evidence of his conceptual immaturity. Thus, a far-reaching correspondence was postulated between the child's thought and his drawing.

Young Children's Sculpture and Drawing

The most detailed analysis of the development of representational thought was made by Piaget, who addressed himself in a series of studies to the growth of the symbolic function in the child. According to Piaget, the mental image plays an important role in the development of representational thought. He postulates that it provides the link between the genetically earlier perceptual processes and later, representational ones. The perception of an object is bound to its immediate presence in the visual field; representation implies the capacity to evoke absent realities. It is the mental image or the symbol which represents the missing object, while its meaning is supplied by thought. Piaget believes that the mental image is the continuation and product of the child's *imitative activity,* which develops during the sensory motor period, and that the image constitutes a kind of internal copy of the object, closely resembling it. Between the ages of two and seven, the child's perception of objects is fairly accurate, while the perceptual (imitative) activity which constitutes the image is not yet fully developed and yields a relatively static mental image.

Piaget considers drawing a special case of imitation, closely related to the mental image, providing as it were a kind of index of the image. Up to the age of seven, graphic imitation of a model succeeds only insofar as the visual model is understood. Faulty imitations are the result of rigid mental images, incapable of analysis. This attempt to relate childish drawings to the immature quality of the mental image raises a number of questions, primarily with regard to the representational models developed in tasks other than drawing, for example, in playdough, with puzzle parts, on dictation, and on completion tasks. Simultaneous construction of several models may point to the existence of multiple mental images or imply a single image which gives rise to different representational models depending on the medium and the task. In either case the mental image does not yield simple printouts, and the drawing should not be viewed as a direct index of the mental image, whether static, immature, or deficient. Moreover, copying a mental image is no easier than copying the real object as Metz's study of eidetic children indicates (Metz, 1929). These subjects, whose mental imagery was as vivid and detailed as the percept of the original scene, drew the same childish drawings as youngsters equipped with poorer mental images.

Traditionally, the term imitation has been applied to a wide range of behavioral situations in which an individual copies or closely matches the behavior of a model. Even casual analysis, however, reveals that the common use of the term hides considerable differences in types of behavior and presumably in the underlying psychological processes: it applies to sensory motor actions as well as to representations of objects and actions. Piaget, for example, has offered detailed and perceptive accounts of the imitative behaviors which he elicited in his children. During the second year of life in particular the child makes great progress in the ability to imitate actions.

Imitation on the sensory motor level requires the accurate perception of an action, gesture, or sound and the ability to match the action as closely as possible and perform it on or with the child's own body. In order to be successful, imitation requires the construction of correspondences. Imitation of such sensory motor events is feasible so long as the medium or vehicle of action is the same for both model and imitator. A gesture such as slapping the thigh, nodding the head, or scratching the cheek lends itself to fairly accurate imitation precisely because the medium of action is the same.

Young Children's Sculpture and Drawing

In attempting to represent objects through drawing
or modeling the provision that imitation occur in
the same medium cannot be fulfilled; neither object
nor action can be duplicated with imitative gestures.
Instead, the young artist has to construct a spatial
representational framework consisting of horizontal
and vertical coordinates and evolve special graphic
and plastic techniques that will enable him to
depict objects of considerable complexity. Unlike
the perception of a gesture, which is a relatively
holistic event, representation is sequential, involving
a series of steps that have to be more closely
coordinated than the single sweeping motion of
imitative action.

Both sensory motor imitation and representation
reflect a desire to create a likeness of the model. In
the former, however, the aim is to achieve a very
close approximation, possibly identical behavior,
while in the latter the aim is to create structural and
dynamic equivalences. Successful caricatures and
pantomimes illustrate the power of such equivalents
to evoke the absent object and its actions. The mime
conjures visual images of striking reality without
necessarily duplicating realistic movements (Simmel,
1972). Imitation, in the strict sense of making an
exact copy based on identical elements, apparently
is only possible when the object to be copied is a
"representation," as is the case with two-dimensional
geometric figures to be copied on paper—or with
the snowman figures of this study (Chapter 6).

The ambition to copy nature is historically and
developmentally a late phenomenon. Unlike the
toddler of the sensory-motor period, who closely
observes the model in order to imitate its actions,
the three- or four-year-old neither studies the model
in an attempt to imitate it nor tries to copy an
internal model as suggested by Eng (1931) and
Piaget (1951). The three- to five-year-old youngster

has neither ambition, interest, or technical means for dealing with perspective distortions, undoing as it were the perceptual constancies of size and shape. To wonder why the child's drawing does not conform to realistic norms is clearly the wrong kind of question. Aside from the highly technical conception and skill necessary for the creation of an "illusion" of reality, the notion of making an exact copy has not yet occurred to the child. The four-year-old has difficulty copying geometric designs other than the circle and the square, though his representation of a person already bears an unmistakable likeness to a man. What the child ends up doing, and this seems a spontaneous phenomenon, is to render on paper or create in playdough simple forms which represent some of the structural characteristics of the object. These forms reflect his interpretation of his experience with the object in the particular medium. For representational purposes, his visual experience yields the most useful information about an object; and when the product of his labors is finished it requires further visual inspection and confirmation.

With the recognition that visual representation need not replicate all aspects of an object, omissions lose their ominous significance. Representation implies abstraction and simplification (Arnheim, 1954), while duplication demands precision, attention to detail and to multiple relationships, a developed spatial framework, and the concept of measurement (Piaget and Inhelder, 1956). Progress in the ability to copy geometric figures parallels to some extent the increasingly stringent demands of "likeness" which the child sets for himself, advancing from the early simple forms of equivalence to more complex and mutually regulated ones.

The foregoing reflections expose the inadequacy of the concept of imitation to account for representational achievement. Let us now consider the relationships between symbolic play and children's art. Unlike imitation, which in Piaget's system is synonymous with the tendency to accommodate to the object, symbolic play tends to transform the object in line with the child's emotional needs. Consequently, accommodation to the object may be minimal. The symbol-object is not only the representative of the signified, but also its substitute. For example, the child may use a shell to represent a cat, but during play the shell ceases to stand for the class of cats and becomes momentarily a cat (Piaget, 1951). In play, unlike conceptual thought, the meaning of the symbol is transient and Piaget considers symbolic play in its extreme form as undisciplined and nonadaptive thought, pure egocentric thought bent on satisfying the whims of the ego. While the distorting aspect of symbolic play has received due recognition by Piaget, it is important to point out its "as if" character, the make-believe pretense which is maintained throughout the play situation without ever being mistaken for reality. In this respect the pretense of play is similar to the child's recognition that his representation merely "stands" for the real thing. Both symbolic play and art represent an aspect of reality, and create equivalences for reality, symbolizing salient attributes of objects and their function. In drawing and modeling visual aspects of the object predominate, while in symbolic play visual, auditory, and kinesthetic characteristics interact with personal meanings to create the highly satisfying symbolic plays of childhood.

The symbolic play of three- and four-year-olds makes use of substitutes, whose likeness to the object is only minimal. A stick between the legs coupled with a galloping motion transforms stick and child into horse and rider. This is reminiscent of the prerepresentational devices of romancing and imitative action typical of an early phase of graphic

Overview

and plastic representation. Their main function is to compensate for the first global and inarticulate forms and to achieve, with the help of playful narratives and corrective interpretations, an imaginative transformation of the object.

In play as well as in representation, the early symbols are of a very general nature. In drawing, the circle can represent almost any part of the human; in play, objects easily substitute one for another. Even at these early stages, however, there are limits to substitutability. A shell, a pebble, or any other indefinite form can substitute for a cat, but objects of well-defined structure and function, such as a doll, a crib, or a house, cannot.

Thus, in their origins symbolic play and the visual arts seem to share a number of characteristics. Representation begins with the child's playful exploration of the medium and its symbolic transformation, and comes increasingly under the domination of the visual attributes of the object, recreating its structural and dynamic characteristics. The link with symbolic representation, however, is never completely lost.

The results of our investigation of children's representation of the human figure demand a radical reformulation of the relation between representation and cognition. The traditional assumption, that the child's representational model stands in a one-to-one correspondence with his concept of the object, has proven untenable, given the multiple models which he evolves, depending on the task and the medium. The "graphic model" in playdough illustrates this well. When the child adopts this method of construction, he outlines his figure with thin strips of dough, that is, he adopts a two-dimensional linear model, taken from drawing. In this case the graphic model overrules the child's basically

three-dimensional percept and concept of a man.
Clearly the two-dimensional playdough figure reflects
methods and procedures invented by the child for
the paper and pencil medium rather than his concept
of a man.

Representation implies abstraction and does not
proceed via piecemeal replication. The young child
is under no compulsion to conform to a "realistic"
standard of representation and to include all the
object's details. He has no desire to "copy" reality;
his lines and circles are his own inventions, and
not given to him in the object. Once he has mastered
such simple but expressive forms as the circle and
the line, the child's explorations yield the first global
human, or tadpole man. These initial organized
representations require a sustained effort which can
be quite exhausting for the three- and four-year-old,
reinforcing the tendency to limit the representation
to its bare essentials. Above all, the youngster feels
free either to include a feature or to leave it out;
a certain playfulness characterizes his early efforts,
and his general attitude implies that the figure,
though far from perfect, will do. Thus, early
productions reflect a child's inexperience with
representational media, his slow discovery of forms,
emphasis on action, and quick satisfaction with
crude form-symbols as well as the youngster's
playfulness and willingness to simplify and
economize.

The older, more experienced child includes more
details in his representation, precisely because he
draws the main outlines with greater ease, in fact
quite effortlessly. Gradually the child becomes more
"task"-oriented, and planful action subordinates
imagination and playful action to the demands of
task and medium. The youngster no longer relies
on verbal interpretations to make sense of his

Overview

accidental products. He now successfully fits the figure to his more rigorous standards of correct representation.

We have witnessed a remarkable change in the child's requirements of representational forms. In the beginning the circle stands for thing-in-general, and the circle with features represents the human. The child at this stage may add further details, but these are considered merely "pretty" and not essential. A few months later the tadpole figure represents the whole man, though a separate trunk is not delineated. Between four and six years the figure shows further differentiation of parts, and the relation of size, proportion, and position is gradually taken into account. A very similar development, from a global to a differentiated figure, can be observed in modeling.

Symbolic play is an important source of creative activity, and the young child's attempts to eliminate contradictions and inconsistencies by renaming, by redefining, and by playful and narrative procedures illustrate this well. The older child, who has acquired representational concepts, models, and skills, can now adequately express his intention in drawing and modeling without relying on verbal transformations of the figure; symbolic representation takes new forms. Perhaps the child is always caught between two opposing attitudes, between the inherent need for ordered, simple, and meaningful representation and the playfulness and fluidity typical of what Piaget calls "symbolic activity." Representation moves between these two extremes: the trend toward imitation and the trend toward symbolization in art.

Young Children's Sculpture and Drawing

References   Index

Anati, E. Origins and Evolution of the Camunian
    Civilization. *Journal of World History*, 10, no. 2,
    1967.

Arnheim, R. *Art and Visual Perception.* Berkeley:
    University of California Press, 1954.

—— *Toward a Psychology of Art: Collected Essays.*
    Berkeley: University of California Press, 1966.

Barr-Grossman, T. A Study of the Representational
    Development of the Human Figure in Familial
    Retardates. Unpublished Honors Thesis, Brandeis
    University, 1973.

Bender, L. *Child Psychiatric Techniques.* Springfield, Ill.:
    Charles C. Thomas, 1952.

Buck, J. N. The H-T-P Technique: a Qualitative and
    Quantitative Scoring Manual. *Journal Clinical
    Psychology*, 4: 317–396, 1948.

Burt, C. *Mental and Scholastic Tests.* London: P. S.
    King and Son, 1921.

Eng, H. *The Psychology of Children's Drawings.*
    London: Routledge and Kegan, 1931.

Golomb, C. *The Effects of Models, Media, and
    Instructions on Children's Representation of the
    Human Figure.* Doctoral Dissertation, Brandeis
    University; Ann Arbor, Mich.: University Microfilms,
    no. 69–16, 3–8, 1969.

—— Evolution of the Human Figure in a
    Three-Dimensional Medium. *Developmental
    Psychology*, 6, no. 3: 385–391, 1972.

—— Children's Representation of the Human Figure:
    The Effects of Models, Media, and Instructions.
    Genetic Psychology Monographs, 87: 197–251, 1973.

Goodenough, F. L. *Measurement of Intelligence by
    Drawings.* New York: Harcourt, Brace and World,
    1926.

—— Children's Drawings, in C. Murchison, ed.,
    A Handbook of Child Psychology. Worcester,
    Mass.: Clark University Press, 1931.

—— *Developmental Psychology*, New York:

Appleton Century, 1934.

Hammer, E. F. Projective Drawings, in A. I. Rubin, ed., *Projective Techniques in Personality Assessment.* New York: Springer, 1968.

Harris, D. B. *Children's Drawings as Measures of Intellectual Maturity.* New York: Harcourt, Brace and World, 1963.

Kellogg, R. *What Children Scribble and Why.* Palo Alto: National Press Books, 1959.

―― *Analyzing Children's Art.* Palo Alto: National Press Books, 1969.

Kerschensteiner, D. G. *Die Entwicklung der zeichnerischen Begabung.* Munich: Gerber, 1905.

Koppitz, E. M. *Psychological Evaluation of Children's Human Figure Drawings.* New York: Grune and Stratton, 1968.

Krötzsch, W. *Rhythmus und Form in der freien Kinderzeichnung.* Leipzig: A. Haase, 1917.

Lukens, H. A Study of Children's Drawings in the Early Years. *Pedagogical Seminary,* 4, no. 1: 79–110, 1896.

Luquet, G. H. *Les Dessins d'un enfant.* Paris: F. Alcan, 1913.

―― Le Dessin enfantin. Paris: F. Alcan, 1927.

Machover, K. *Personality Projection in the Drawings of the Human Figure.* Springfield, Ill.: Charles C. Thomas, 1949.

―― Human Figure Drawings of Children. *Journal of Projective Techniques,* 17, no. 1: 85–91, 1953.

Meili-Dworetzki, G. *Das Bild Des Menschen in der Vorstellung und Darstellung des Kleinkindes.* Bern: Hans Huber, 1957.

Metz, P. *Die eidetische Anlage der Jugendlichen in iher Beziehung zur künstlerischen Gestaltung.* Langensalza: H. Beyer and Sons, 1929.

Piaget, J. *The Language and Thought of the Child.* New York: Harcourt, Brace, 1926.

―― *Play, Dreams, and Imitation in Childhood.* New York: W. W. Norton, 1951.

―― and B. Inhelder, *The Child's Conception of Space.* London: Routledge, Kegan Paul, 1956.

―― and B. Inhelder, *The Psychology of the Child.* New York: Basic Books, 1969.

Young Children's Sculpture and Drawing

———— and B. Inhelder, *Mental Imagery in the Child.*
New York: Basic Books, 1971.

Ricci, C. *L'Arte dei Bambini.* Bologna: N. Zanichelli,
1887.

Roback, H. B. Human Figure Drawings: Their Utility in
the Clinical Psychologist's Armamentarium for
Personality Assessment. *Psychological Bulletin,*
70, no. 1: 1–19, 1968.

Schilder, P. *The Image and Appearance of the Human
Body.* New York: International Universities
Press, 1959 (1935).

Simmel, M. L. Mime and Reason: Notes on the Creation
of the Perceptual Object. *Journal of Aesthetics
and Art Criticism,* 31, no. 2: 193–200, 1972.

Sully, J. *Studies of Childhood.* London: Appleton, 1896.
———— *Studies of Childhood,* revised edition. London:
Appleton, 1910.

Swensen, E. H. Empirical Evaluations of Human Figure
Drawings: 1957–1966. *Psychological Bulletin,*
70, no. 1: 20–44, 1968.

Werner, H. *Comparative Psychology of Mental
Development.* Chicago: Follett, 1948.